FORTY
TO A CLOSER WALK
WITH GOD

THE PRACTICE OF
CENTERING PRAYER

J. DAVID MUYSKENS

UPPER
ROOM BOOKS®
NASHVILLE

FORTY DAYS TO A CLOSER WALK WITH GOD
The Practice of Centering Prayer
© 2006 by J. David Muyskens
All rights reserved.

Cover design: Bruce Gore/Gore Studio
Cover art: St. Catherine's Labyrinth by Jan L. Richardson © 2003
   www.janrichardson.com

Library of Congress Cataloging-in-Publication
Muyskens, J. David, 1934–
   Forty days to a closer walk with God: the practice of centering prayer / J. David Muyskens.
      p. cm.
   Includes bibliographical references (p. 137).
   ISBN-13: 978-0-8358-9904-8
   1. Contemplation. 2. Prayer—Christianity. I. Title.
   BV5091.C7M89 2006
   248.3'4—dc22

                                        2006023036

Printed in the United States of America

More praise for

FORTY DAYS TO A CLOSER WALK WITH GOD

I am deeply impressed with this informative and insightful book inspired by David Muyskens' life-changing experience of Centering Prayer. Drawing from a rich variety of both Catholic and Protestant spiritual resources, plus daily contemplative prayer practices and meditations on scripture, he leads us gently into an ever-deepening friendship with God.

—DON POSTEMA
Emeritus Campus Pastor
Campus Chapel, University of Michigan, Ann Arbor

This book offers the reader new to contemplative prayer an accessible, personally oriented way of living into such prayer over a forty-day period. It is full of insightful scriptural, historical, and biographical references that help the reader enter into Christian contemplative tradition and practice.

—TILDEN EDWARDS
Founder and Senior Fellow
Shalem Institute for Spiritual Formation

Our contemporary age hungers for greater depth and wholeness that is available in contemplative Christian spirituality. Muyskens invites his readers to discover and experience the healing presence and indwelling intimacy of our Triune God through Centering Prayer. This practical and balanced guide will be a welcome resource for those who are seeking to become more attentive to God's gracious presence and responsive to the needs of others.

—TOM SCHWANDA
Associate Professor of Christian Formation and Ministry
Wheaton College, Wheaton, Illinois

CONTENTS

ACKNOWLEDGMENTS

I THANK MY WIFE, DONNA, for her support and encouragement and for allowing me long hours for writing.

I have very much appreciated the encouragement of Thomas Keating throughout the process of writing this book.

Thanks to Gail Fitzpatrick-Hopler, president of Contemplative Outreach and to Carl Arico, vice president of Contemplative Outreach, for reading the manuscript and supporting its publication.

I deeply appreciate the friends who have read early drafts and have offered their suggestions: Elaine Tetreault, Maria Owens, Carole Vander Pols, Molly Keating, John Topliff, and Linda Koch. Thanks to Carol Rottman for help given through her writing class. I thank my daughter Julia Ostendorf for her suggestions. I am grateful to members of the spiritual disciplines class of New Brunswick Theological Seminary for their feedback. I value the suggestions of the other members of The Well writers' group: Cynthia Beach, Marjo Jordan, Barbara Schultze, Ruth Romeyn, and Mary Zwaanstra.

I thank JoAnn Miller, Lynne Deming, and Rita Collett, Upper Room Books editors, for their expert editorial assistance and counsel.

And thanks to the members of an adult education class at Church of the Servant who gave the material a "trial run" led by Carole Vander Pols and me. Among them were Jill Frazee-Eitman, Elaine Hoekstra, Robbie Keech, Ruth Lemmenes, J. Annette Nordyke, Pam and Harry Plantinga, Ruth Schoff, Stephanie Sandberg, and Nancy Van Baak.

PREFACE

I INVITE YOU TO COME with me on a journey filled with discovery and challenge, sustained always by the intimate love of our divine Companion. I am confident that taking time for the daily readings and prayer this book suggests will bring you to a deeper love of God because you will learn a method of prayer that is centered in God. It consents to the love God has for you. The method, called Centering Prayer, will enable you to take at least a few minutes of your day simply to be in God's loving embrace, free from the noise and tension of the world around you. And you will discover how to deal with the hardest part of silent prayer: the many thoughts that arise from within. Centering Prayer goes deeper than words can express and beyond thought and imagination. It offers a way to enter the heart of God.

The words from Psalm 46 are familiar: "Be still, and know that I am God!" Many other biblical texts offer an invitation to silence and a quiet consent to God's indwelling presence. Each of the forty days' readings highlights a biblical passage that calls you to contemplative prayer and contemplative living. The readings, which come from many parts of the Bible, demonstrate Centering Prayer's rootedness in holy scripture.

This book has two purposes. First, to explore a practice of prayer that leads to deep communion with God. Second, to encourage a way of life motivated by the divine Presence at the center of your being.

When Jesus talked with the woman at the well in Samaria, he spoke of an inner spring from which the living water of the Spirit flows. Centering Prayer flows from that deep place into a centered life.

Your life can be chaotic, scattered, unfocused. In prayer you consent to a new orientation. Centering Prayer reorients you to your true center, a surrender to the inward centripetal pull of Christ who dwells within.

With that orientation, another pull exerts itself, a centrifugal movement outward. You live out of the center, extending love to others, caring for creation, working for justice and peace. You live from the inside out, directed by Christ to serve.

The prayer for the inner journey is "that you may be strengthened in your inner being . . . that Christ may dwell in your hearts" (Eph. 3:16, 17). That's the centripetal work of the Spirit drawing you into communion with God. Then the centrifugal force directs you into a life of love: "Lead a life worthy of the calling to which you have been called, with all humility and gentleness, with patience, bearing with one another in love" (Eph. 4:1-2). The love and courage for service spin out of a deep relationship with the triune God. This deeply private prayer will not be private at all; it leads to unity with your Creator and all creation.

In Centering Prayer you yield to the One who is your true center. A daily practice of Centering Prayer will not take the place of other forms of prayer, praise, thanksgiving, confession, and petition; it will enhance them. This book will help you practice Centering Prayer and a way of praying with scripture. In the practice of Centering Prayer you yield to the One who is your true center. You open your heart to receive the gift of contemplative prayer.

Following the suggestions for scriptural meditation given for each day, you will use the ancient method of praying with scripture known as *lectio divina*, literally "divine reading." In this method, developed in early Christian history, you read scripture to listen for a word from God. You let your attention be drawn to one word or phrase that emerges. Meditation on that word or phrase follows, and you reflect on the meaning of the word for you. From that reflection come your prayers, silent or spoken. This process brings you to contemplation, resting in God. In silent contemplation the word sinks deeply into the subconscious where it can affect your attitudes and behavior. While our fast-paced society tempts us to neglect this silent time, it is here that we realize the love of God most deeply. The Latin words for the four aspects of *lectio divina* are *lectio*, *meditatio*, *oratio*, and *contemplatio*. We can translate them as reading, reflection, response, and rest.

HOW TO READ THIS BOOK

By reading this book straight through, you will gain a broad overview of the practice of Centering Prayer, its biblical background, and its fruit in daily life. I suggest that you take time to read it daily for forty days and follow the exercises for prayer and reading of scripture. To develop a routine, consider establishing a time and place for your daily prayer. You might want to do this the first thing in the morning. You may have another time each day when you can be quiet for about forty minutes. It helps to have a place conducive to prayer where you can have one or more symbols of God's presence; for example, a cross, a picture of Christ, a candle, or a flower. You will need a Bible and a notebook as well as this book. The notebook can be a journal in which you make daily entries that grow out of your meditation. Unless you prefer to sit on the floor, you will need a comfortable chair (but not too comfortable).

You might also consider reading this book with a group. You do the daily reading and exercises and then meet with a group once a week to share your reflections and hear what other group members are receiving. Group use encourages the profound experience of being in silent prayer with others. If the group is using the book in Lent, Ash Wednesday can be the first day and the group meetings held on Sundays. (The forty days of Lent do not include Sundays.) Suggestions for group meetings begin on page 121.

1   THE GIFT OF PRAYER

> Thus said the Lord GOD, the Holy One of Israel:
> In returning and rest you shall be saved;
>> in quietness and in trust shall be your strength.
>
> —Isaiah 30:15

The oilcloth-covered table was set, the fragrance of the freshly cooked food increasing our appetite. But even if it meant that food got a little colder, we children could not take a bite until Dad prayed and asked for God's blessing. After sharing the meal, before any of us could leave the table, Dad read scripture and Mother gave thanks. So from day one I knew the importance of prayer. I heard grandparents, uncles, and aunts pray at the table when we were guests in their homes. My parents taught me bedtime prayers. I witnessed my father praying from the pulpit as pastor on Sundays. At the Wednesday evening prayer meeting many people offered extemporaneous prayer. I learned to pray from my elders. I am thankful for this early grounding in prayer.

The prayer I learned was addressed to the Creator infinitely above and beyond. This great Initiator of the cosmos and Governor of life sat enthroned in grandeur, awesome and majestic. In prayer I could talk to this God of power. I could actually connect and be heard, like reaching a parent when far from home by making a long-distance call. Now I have discovered that prayer can also be a close and personal relationship. In Christ, God has come to us; and we can engage in intimate conversation and loving communion.

God is beyond but also near, transcendent and immanent. Seen not only with telescopic vision but also in the microscopic view of deep intimacy. God is the Source beyond my imagining and also the Lover who is immediately present. God, the Center of all, dwells at the center of my being. So when I am centered, I open the eyes of my heart to perceive God's presence, transcendent in glory and present here and now. I receive the gift of an intimate relationship with God deeper than words can express. I let go of my efforts to reach God and simply rest in the love of the Trinity. I let go of my attachments and surrender myself to Christ. I release whatever thoughts come to me and consent to the Presence and to the restoring action of the Spirit within.

In the quiet of silent prayer I accept the gift of communion with the Holy One. I wait to receive this gift, which comes like a flower blossoming. I cannot force the flower to bloom any faster than it will. I can only express gratitude for the beauty that unfolds.

My prayers of gratitude take many forms. At times I listen for the word of God. At times I speak words of praise, thanksgiving, confession, intercession, and supplication. And at times I am silent, without words, welcoming Christ and his transforming work within.

On a sunny beach we can enjoy the warmth of the sun, absorbing the rays of sunlight as we lie on the sand. In Centering Prayer we bask in the love of God. No danger of skin cancer in this activity! We receive the healing warmth of divine love and the transforming work of Christ.

This gift comes in silence through patient and attentive waiting. "Through the Spirit, by faith, we eagerly wait for the hope of righteousness" (Gal. 5:5). "Be still before the LORD, and wait patiently" (Ps. 37:7). "For God alone my soul waits in silence; from [God] comes my salvation" (Ps. 62:1). We let go of all except God. Our prayer becomes an intimate communion with the One who comes to us in love. It is worth the wait—a gift beyond measure.

PRAYER PRACTICE

As you begin to pray, what is the name of God you commonly choose? The name you use to address God can be a word that helps you stay in an open attitude of silent prayer. You approach and address God and then you go no further; you simply commune with God in a loving relationship for the Centering Prayer period. Later you listen for God's word and make your verbal prayers. For now, you enter silent communion.

I recommend that you begin with at least twenty minutes of Centering Prayer. If that is not possible, try taking as much time as you can. If you start with five minutes a day at first, you can move to ten minutes next week and work your way up to at least twenty.

When a thought comes to you, let go of it for the time being by gently returning to your familiar name for God. Every time you recall that name, it will open your heart to the loving presence of God.

Next read Isaiah 30:15-18. Begin with the prayer, "God, what do you want to say to me?" Read not for information but for formation, not for comprehension but for apprehension, not to think of God but to know God. Allow a word from the reading to speak to you. Meditate on the word that caught your attention. Reflect on the word, asking, "What does the word I am hearing mean for me?" You can begin a daily journal by recording the date, the scripture reference read, the word that caught your attention, and reflective thoughts you receive during meditation. Respond to God in verbal prayer. This you can also write in your journal if you wish. Finally, give yourself a little time simply to rest in God. Take time for contemplation deeper than words. As you leave your place of prayer, take with you the word you received from the reading, as well as the interior silence and calm you have been given.

2   STILL A TEACHER

"Remember, I am with you always, to the end of the age."
—Matthew 28:20

Elfrieda MacIntyre showed me a deeper, life-transforming way of prayer. At the time my practice of prayer consisted of grace at mealtime and, as a minister, leading my congregation in prayer. I had no personal daily discipline of prayer; my practice of prayer was sporadic and occasional.

Elfrieda was ninety-eight years old when we met. Never married, still alert, she had once been a public school teacher. As the appointed pastoral supervisor of her church in Hoboken, New Jersey, I was encouraged by church members to visit Elfrieda in the Pollak Hospital in Jersey City.

Elfrieda's incredible joy made our visits delightful. She expressed interest in any news I brought from the church and anything I had to tell her. She was one of the happiest people I have ever known.

Pollak Hospital was at that time a senior care facility. The building had once been part of a state-of-the-art medical center, providing the best medical care for miles around. Its tall buildings stood out on the Jersey City skyline. By now they had become drab structures.

Elfrieda had none of the things I was striving for—income, retirement fund, a family with well-educated children, car, boat, travel, recognition. The gray walls of Elfrieda's room looked as if they had not been painted for thirty years. In a 15' by 20' room, she lived with three other women. Unwashed windows gave light to one side of the room. Each resident had a corner with a cot, a nightstand, and a chair. Had I been in her place, I would have been quite angry and bitter.

After making a number of visits, I became bold. One day I entered her room to find her sitting in her chair with eyes closed, apparently meditating. I asked her what she was thinking. Elfrieda replied, "I was saying over and over to myself the verse from the Bible: 'Lo, I am with you always, to the end of the age.'"

Now I knew! The presence of Christ gave her joy despite her meager circumstances. God was with her, and assurance filled her soul. Elfrieda knew Jesus' promise, "I am with you always." Quiet recall of that verse took her into a gentle awareness of Christ's presence.

Jesus told his disciples, "I am in my Father, and you in me, and I in you" (John 14:20). The living Christ resides in us. Jesus said, "Abide in me as I abide in you" (John 15:4). Our souls become the dwelling place of God. The apostle Paul taught that we are in Christ, and the Spirit of Christ dwells in us (Rom. 8:11). This key to true happiness is transformation from within by the indwelling Christ.

Over time I came to appreciate the lesson I received from Elfrieda, whose way of prayer opens the soul to the divine indwelling. She practiced contemplative prayer without knowing the word for it. (I did not know it myself at the time.) At age ninety-eight she was still a teacher.

Prayer is more than conversation. Entering a close walk with God will sometimes call for words and sometimes for a simple enjoyment of presence. In silent, contemplative prayer I simply rest in God. Moving beyond verbal conversation, I move into quiet communion.

As a relationship deepens, we no longer need many words to enjoy each other's company. In an intimate relationship, two people value each other's presence, sometimes with words, sometimes in silence.

Prayer can be a deep fulfillment of Jesus' promise to be with us always.

PRAYER PRACTICE

Take twenty minutes to appreciate the gift of Christ's presence. Be in silence; sit comfortably with your back erect so you can relax and yet remain internally alert. Employ the name of God you used yesterday or the name *Jesus* as your prayer word for this period. Whenever a thought arises, instead of following it, gently return to the sacred name.

After this time of silence, turn to Matthew 28:16-20. Let a word emerge from that reading. Listen to what God is saying to you. Enter in your journal the date, text, and what you heard. Offer your prayers in silent thought and written words.

Take a moment to let what you have heard sink in. Bring the awareness of Christ with you into every moment.

3   THE INNER FLAME OF THE SPIRIT

The human spirit is the lamp of the LORD.

—Proverbs 20:27

When winter comes in western Michigan where I live, I get out my warm coat and check the gas furnace of our home. When the thermostat calls for more heat, the furnace sends fuel into the chamber where the pilot light burns. With oxygen from the air, the gas burns brightly, warming air that is then blown throughout the house.

Each of us has a God-given pilot light. Created in the image of God, we have a built-in longing for God. That longing can be ignited into a burning love for God. Our hearts can burn within us as did the hearts of two disciples on the way to Emmaus when the risen Christ joined them.

As John Wesley heard the words of Luther's preface to Romans, his heart was "strangely warmed." The message of God's love and grace in Christ gave him assurance of his salvation. The word of scripture was fuel for his soul. That word catches fire when nourished by the oxygen of the Spirit. The breath of God brought Adam, Eve, and all humanity to life and resurrected the dry bones in Ezekiel's vision. The wind of the Spirit brought power and courage to the disciples of Jesus at Pentecost. The Spirit blowing in us brings the flame of life and love to a bright burning.

John of the Cross, Spanish reformer of his Carmelite community in the mid- to late-1500s, wrote about the Holy Spirit as the "Living Flame of Love." He said,

> This flame the soul feels within it, not only as a fire that has consumed and transformed it in sweet love, but also as a fire which burns within it and sends out flame. . . . The enkindling of love, wherein the will of the soul is united, and it loves most deeply, being made one with that flame in love.[1]

Prayer expresses our willingness to have the flame within rekindled. The quiet time allows the inner flame to burn brightly and transform us. In Centering Prayer we let go of everything and choose a word that expresses our consent to God's presence and action within. As thoughts draw us away from communion with God, we return to that prayer word as a way of turning again to God. Using that word we stay with our desire to receive the loving presence and healing action of Christ. We disregard thoughts that can hinder the fire within. We allow the love of Christ to burn away the resistance and obstacles to communion with God. We are purged of desires that so often draw us away from God.

The daily practice of prayer requires discipline. The first challenge is to sit down. I am a jogger. I know the truth of the saying that the hardest part of jogging is to get out the door. We have to find the time and actually exercise. The practice of Centering Prayer requires regular daily prayer time; it is not easy, but we make time for what is important.

As we take time for prayer and scripture, the soul burns, not for the self but for God. We surrender to Christ. Then the glow within radiates with love, joy, and peace.

PRAYER PRACTICE

Open your heart to let the gentle breeze of the Spirit fan the flame of love for God within you. Take the same prayer word you have used or another as a symbol of your intention to consent to God's presence and action within. Take twenty minutes to remain open to the love of God. You may use a timer or glance at a clock as needed. As thoughts come, let go of them by returning to your prayer word. Close your time of silence with a prayer of thanksgiving.

Read Acts 2:1-4. Let a word stand out from this reading. Reflect on it. Ask what that word means for you. Notice your emotions in response to that word. What is being asked of you to let the fire of the Spirit ignite your heart?

Write in your journal the date, text, word given, and your reflections. Ask for God's help and blessing for yourself and for others who come to your attention as you remain in quiet. Take the word you received and the warmth of God's love with you as you go about your activities.

4 DIMENSIONS OF PRAYER

Be still before the LORD, and wait patiently for him.

—Psalm 37:7

The first dimension of prayer is God's love for us. Before we utter a word, the Spirit puts in our hearts a desire to communicate with the Source of our being. God has given us life and love. In prayer we gratefully receive these gifts. We begin prayer with listening, receiving the word expressed most eloquently in Jesus Christ.

In the second dimension of prayer we respond. In distress we call out for help and in gratitude offer our thanksgiving. Receiving divine love, we return our praise. We confess our sin and make petition. We talk to God, expressing the love we have because God first loved us.

The third dimension of prayer is intimate communion. The love and grace of the Holy One draws us into the embrace of pure love. This is the dimension of prayer too often ignored. God desires to give the gift of contemplation. With a method such as Centering Prayer we can be open to receive this gift.

We cannot know what it is like to take a walk in the woods until we do it. We can imagine it, read about it, and look at pictures. But we have to experience it for ourselves to know what it is really like. Only in the woods can we know the awesome majesty of the tall trees, the inspiration of light rays that stream in through the gaps in their leaves, the fragrance of wildflowers and the scent of pine. Only there can we feel the vibrancy of the life that grows on the floor of the forest reaching upward toward the light that breaks through the canopy overhead. The woods bear witness to the cycle of life and death as decaying fallen trees become fertile soil to nurture new life. By entering the woods and walking the trail we may experience all that.

We cannot know what it is like to sail until we actually get in a sailboat. We can look on as an observer and get some idea of it. But knowing the feel of moving across the water requires that we get in the boat and on the water. Only then will we experience the power of the wind. Only as we engage in the attentiveness required to keep the tiller at the angle needed to catch wind in the sails and move at optimum speed do we know the thrill of sailing.

In the spiritual life only as we become engaged with the Holy One does knowledge of the transforming power of the indwelling Christ, the profound intimacy of the love of God, and the joy of living by the Spirit come to us. We cannot know what contemplative prayer is until we willingly receive the gift.

We receive the gift of divine presence as we let go of our efforts and accept the love of Christ. Not with human effort or language but by the Spirit the gift is given. Beyond words, symbols, and feelings the Spirit gives us an intimate relationship with God.

The story is told of a Jewish peasant who became so absorbed in his work in the field that he did not notice that the sun had gone down. It was the eve of Passover, and he was not allowed to travel after sunset. So he spent the night in the field. At sunrise his rabbi came walking through the field and said to the peasant, "Your family missed you last night." With a sigh the peasant explained what had happened.

"Well," said the rabbi, "I hope you at least said the appointed prayers."

"No," the peasant replied, "that's the worst of it. I was so upset that I could not remember the words."

"Then how did you pass the holy evening?" asked the rabbi.

"I recited my alphabet," said the peasant, "and I trusted God to form the words."

We can trust God to form the words in us when we pray. We can trust God to give us the deep desires of the heart that are consistent with the divine will. Without language we can allow the Spirit to pray in us. "The Spirit helps us in our weakness; for we do not know how to pray as we ought, but that very Spirit intercedes with sighs too deep for words" (Rom. 8:26). God knows our needs. In prayer our hearts join with every desire in God's heart for us and for our world. In Centering Prayer this happens in silence without words. In other times of prayer we put words to our needs as the Spirit makes us aware of them.

PRAYER PRACTICE

Sitting erect, become quiet by breathing deeply. As you take a deep breath, imagine yourself welcoming the presence of the Spirit of God. As you exhale, let go of everything that hinders you from receiving the divine presence. Take your favorite name of God or another word that symbolizes your deep consent to the Spirit within you. As thoughts come to you, return to that sacred word as a way of turning again to be with God in faith and love. Enter twenty minutes of silence with that word. Close this time of silence with the Lord's Prayer.

Read Psalm 37:1-7. Let a word emerge from the reading. As you meditate on it, what are you feeling? Write in your journal the date, text, word given, and what God is saying to you. Offer prayers of thanksgiving and petition. Then take a few minutes to rest in the silence, preparing yourself to remain in a prayerful, contemplative mood as you go about your next responsibilities.

5   Letting God Set the Pace

"Be still, and know that I am God!"

—Psalm 46:10

I felt driven to be an activist. I believed that we serve the Lord through action. I believed that Christ came to transform the world and that I was called to help. So I worked hard to foster the church's impact on society.

Working hard "for God," I did not attend to what God was doing, nor did I wait on God to show me how to participate. To me those who spent time in contemplation were wasting time, engaged in escapism, and hiding from the problems of the world. They were avoiding reality, not finding it.

I got my first taste of contemplative prayer when I attended a retreat led by James Fenhagen that encouraged the repetition of a phrase from Psalm 46, "Be still, and know that I am God!" Quiet repetition of that verse helped me find a deeper awareness of God.

Drawn to this quiet way of prayer on a sporadic basis, I found it calming and renewing; but I continued my busy pace of urban ministry. I participated in a political reform movement. I led a coffeehouse ministry and a family life group. In the summer I directed a six-week program for children in the city. Leading a church in a city with a growing number of immigrants, I didn't take much time for prayer.

When I moved to a historic downtown church in another city, I continued to lead the congregation in outreach. I joined a group of people working to effect change in the development of the community around the church, paying attention to the poor threatened by economic development, working for preservation of the neighborhood and the historic buildings in it. I represented the church in a nonprofit corporation for affordable housing. I worked hard as the pastor of an urban church challenged by population changes and growing secularism.

By the fall of 1984, chest and abdominal pains became too severe to ignore, so I made doctors' appointments. One afternoon, feeling I could not wait for appointments weeks away on the calendar, I went to the emergency room of a hospital. I underwent various tests, received an electrocardiogram, and was asked my medical history. Then I lay on the gurney waiting for word of what was wrong. After a while a doctor came over to me and asked, "Are you trying to do it all yourself?"

My symptoms were caused by stress. The doctor's question spoke prophetically to me. It called for change. I had not been seeking God's guidance and power. I *was* trying to do it myself. I resigned from two committees, added fiber to my diet, and began jogging. But the most important change I made was to begin a regular practice of prayer.

Don Postema's book *Space for God: The Study and Practice of Prayer and Spirituality* was just off the press. I devoured it. I began to spend early morning time with quiet repetition of phrases like "I belong to God" and the Jesus Prayer: "Lord Jesus Christ, have mercy on me." I meditated on scripture and prayed.

Postema suggested ways to spend daily time with God. A campus pastor at the University of Michigan in Ann Arbor, Michigan, Postema had spent a sabbatical year with Henri Nouwen at Yale Divinity School. Encouraged by Nouwen, Postema added the rich tradition of contemplative prayer from the desert people of early Christian history and the monastics and mystics of the ages to his Reformed theology. That addition resulted in a spirituality of gratitude with which I resonated.

My spiritual roots grew out of a piety of gratitude for the grace of God. In response to our salvation the Heidelberg Catechism says we "with our whole life . . . may show ourselves grateful to God" (Question 86, The Heidelberg Catechism, 1563). John Calvin wrote his *Institutes* to inspire a piety of reverence and love of God.[1] I felt that the renewed interest in prayer and prayerful living as expressed in Postema's book revived the pietism my grandparents had brought from the Netherlands.

I began to realize the amount of prayer it took to undergird ministry. Unless I sought God's guidance and strength, I would soon be stressed out or burned out.

In 1987 Eugene H. Peterson published a book called *Working the Angles: The Shape of Pastoral Integrity*, which describes the task of ministry and how to remain vital in it. This book helped me put my work into focus. My primary task was not to be chief executive officer of a nonprofit corporation but to be a spiritual leader by drawing people's attention to God. Of course, to do that, I myself had to be attentive to God. I learned Peterson's "trigonometry" of pastoral ministry with the triangle's visible sides of preaching, teaching and administration. Support for the sides comes from the three angles: scripture, prayer, and spiritual direction.

After hearing Peterson speak at a pastors' conference in Minneapolis in July 1989, I found a spiritual director to help me in my practice of prayer, one of the Sisters of the Cenacle. She helped me stick to my discipline of daily prayer, which brought about not only an awareness of God in the time of prayer but an increased attentiveness to God the rest of the time.

PRAYER PRACTICE

Settle in your posture and place for prayer. Recall the words of the psalm, "Be still, and know that I am God!" Let yourself enter the stillness in which you can receive the gift of a deep awareness of God. Ask the Holy Spirit to give you a word that expresses your intention to consent to God's presence and action within. It may be the same word you used yesterday. Gently introduce that word as you enter twenty minutes of silence, simply opening your heart to God. Whenever you begin to think about anything, gently return to that word, renewing your intention to be with God in faith and love. Close the period of wordless prayer with words of thanksgiving.

Read Psalm 46. Let a word or short phrase speak to you. Listen to what the Spirit is saying to you through that word. Recall a time of awakening when you felt the call to a deeper relationship with God. Write your reflections and prayer response. Remain for a few minutes in quiet gratitude. Take with you the word you have been given.

6   IMAGE OF GOD

"Abide in me as I abide in you."

—John 15:4

We cannot develop a close relationship with God if we have a distorted image of God. If we think God is uninvolved in daily events, then we will not see God's activity in what happens. If we see God as being very remote, then personal communication is impossible. If we perceive God as a judge whom we appease with good behavior or as a policeman who watches for our every offense, we will believe that God cannot love us.

God is far greater than anything we can imagine. Yet, through Jesus, we can know the loving nature of our Creator. Scripture tells us God is love and that God delights in us. God comes to us and dwells in us.

As a young person I believed in God. As a teenager one sunny day in my grandmother's backyard, I was filled with gratitude for the gift of faith. Faith seemed required for the courage to live. Later as a young man, I experienced a transcendent moment as I walked across the front lawn of the church I pastored. An overwhelming feeling gave me the thought, *I love God*. But God still existed far above and beyond me.

Now as I began to learn more about contemplatives and mystics, I discovered how much they experienced God to be dwelling within. This I found hard to understand. I remember telling my spiritual director that while I acknowledged the testimony of people who felt God dwelt within them, I did not feel that. Actually by the internal work of the Spirit, I was beginning to realize the gift of the indwelling Christ. In time Jesus' words came alive: "Abide in me as I abide in you." I resonated the prayer that we be "filled with all the fullness of God" (Eph. 3:19). Gradually, through scripture, prayer, and the patient companionship of my spiritual director, I became conscious of the divine indwelling.

Since I had found spiritual direction helpful, I felt called to offer spiritual direction to others. I participated in the Spiritual Guidance Program of the Shalem Institute for Spiritual Formation. Through the Shalem program I learned the value of silent time with God, time in God's presence.

With the help of my spiritual director and the Shalem program, my practice of prayer deepened. I gave blocks of time every morning to prayer. This early morning prayer time included reading scripture, meditation and journaling, being silent with God, and then engaging in intercession for those whose needs had come to my attention.

Spiritual direction helped me get in touch with my inner self. Prayer became more a matter of the heart for me as I opened myself to God's loving presence and healing work within.

An Eastern legend relates a story about Zacchaeus, who is retired. In his retirement he makes a practice of going for an early morning walk every day. He never tells his wife where he goes on these walks. One day her curiosity gets the better of her. Without his knowing, she follows and watches where he goes. She watches him go to the tree where he first met Jesus. He waters the tree's roots. He pulls up weeds that grow next to the tree. He affectionately strokes the tree.

After returning home his wife reveals that she followed and watched his actions at the tree. She asks him if he did that every morning. "Yes," he said, "that is where I met the One whom my soul loves."

All of us need a daily exercise in which we remember the One our soul loves. The practice will keep that love alive in us.

The place we go for prayer can be significant. Each of us can find a special place: a corner for prayer at home, a quiet chapel or church, a retreat center, a historic site that becomes a meeting point with the Lord.

PRAYER PRACTICE

Be in a quiet place with back erect; settle briefly, and silently become aware of the love of God, allowing that love to fill your heart. Whenever thoughts take you somewhere else, return to a word that says, "I open my heart to your love."

After twenty minutes, read John 15:1-5. Take a word that catches your attention, then listen to what God is saying to you through that word. Write in your journal. Pray for the courage and attentiveness to be aware of Christ's presence in every moment and in everyone you meet.

7   THE METHOD OF CENTERING PRAYER

"Whenever you pray, go into your room and shut the door and pray to your Father who is in secret."

—Matthew 6:6

Jesus said when you pray, don't stand on the street corner so people can see how holy you are. Rather, go into your private room and in secret commune with the One who loves you like a perfect parent. There you spend private time with your "Abba." You enter into prayer with God who can be known by this most intimate name, as we might use the words *dad* or *daddy* or *papa* to speak lovingly with our father. In secret, in silence and solitude, we meet in love. In the deep place of our private self we enter an intimate relationship with the one who is our Creator and our eternal Lover.

In Centering Prayer you choose a word, sometimes called a prayer word, sometimes called a sacred word, that expresses your desire to be in an intimate relationship with God. This word says you intend to enter that secret room of communion with God. It is not a time for thinking or for words but for presence. Whenever a thought kidnaps you from that intention, you return to that word as a way of letting go of the thought and returning to God.

Here are the guidelines of Centering Prayer as stated by Thomas Keating, founder of the Contemplative Outreach network that supports the practice of Centering Prayer:

1. Choose a sacred word as the symbol of your intention to consent to God's presence and action within.

2. Sitting comfortably and with eyes closed, settle briefly and silently introduce the sacred word as the symbol of your consent to God's presence and action within.

3. When engaged with your thoughts, return ever-so-gently to the sacred word.

4. At the end of the prayer period, remain in silence with eyes closed for a couple of minutes.

The first guideline. Ask the Holy Spirit to give you a prayer word that expresses your desire to be with God in faith and love. You may be led to use your most familiar name for God. Some examples may include the following: God, Jesus, Father, Abba, Mother, Lord, Spirit. Jesus' word was *Abba.* The early church used the name of Jesus when approaching God.

You may be led to choose another word that expresses, for you, your desire to be in communion with God. Such a word could be *love, amor, peace, faith, trust, grace, mercy, joy, silence, stillness, calm, open, presence, yes, amen.*

Having chosen a sacred word, you use it for the entire period of Centering Prayer. In time one word will become second nature for you. As the author of *The Cloud of Unknowing* said, your sacred word becomes attached to your heart.[1]

We call a symbol sacred because it points to God. As an icon is a window, so a sacred symbol is transparent to the reality it represents. In Centering Prayer we do not focus on the sacred symbol itself but use it to turn our attention to God. Its sacredness does not reside in any magical powers or special value of its own but only in its expression of our turning to God.

In the years I have practiced Centering Prayer, I have had only two prayer words. First I used the word *Spirit* as a familiar name for God. Later I changed to *presence*, which symbolizes my consent to the presence of the Trinity and of my being present. I have thought about changing it again, but this word has become so much a part of my subconscious it keeps coming back. It is not a matter of thinking about the word and what it means but using it as a way to free me from all thought. A simple, short word works best. Avoid anything complicated or a word that has so many connotations that it will take you into more tangents of thought.

At times I do not need the word. I let go of it. Just a gentle turning to God is enough.

PRAYER PRACTICE

Use a sacred word you have already chosen or take a little time to ask the Holy Spirit to give you the prayer word for your Centering Prayer time. Let the word emerge from deep within you as you wait on the Spirit's prompting. Gently introduce that word as you begin twenty minutes of

Centering Prayer. With that one word you state your intention to consent to God's presence and action. When you find yourself thinking about something, let go of that thought by returning to your sacred word. This is not a violent or forced action but a very gentle one. Don't change the prayer word during the course of the twenty minutes. Close the twenty minutes with thanksgiving.

Read Matthew 6:5-6. Listen for what God is saying to you. What strikes you in this teaching of Jesus on prayer? Where and when can you be in secret communion with the Lover of your soul? Write in your journal about your experience in prayer. Pray for God's continued guidance. Take the divine presence you have been given into the rest of life.

8   More Guidelines

"Do not heap up empty phrases."

—Matthew 6:7

The second guideline. This guideline has to do with posture and how you begin the Centering Prayer period. Sitting in an erect position is probably the best posture for most of us. If you are limber, sitting on the floor may be good. Standing and kneeling are biblical postures for prayer, but they may not be suitable for twenty to thirty minutes. So sitting in a chair is fine. One rule most of us find important is to have the spine straight. When the back is erect the head rests more comfortably than if you lean too much forward or backward. With the spine straight you can be in a restful position but not so relaxed as to fall asleep. When in a chair, plant both feet on the floor to feel grounded. Crossed legs require readjustment of position every few minutes because some circulation gets cut off. Hands can be held in a gesture of openness or in whatever position is comfortable.

If agitated or anxious, you may want to calm yourself as you approach the Centering Prayer period by taking some deep breaths. Make each inhalation an act of receiving the love of God and each exhalation an act of letting go of all that keeps you from God. Or you can choose another way of relaxing body and mind: do some stretching, read a psalm. Then as you sit in your posture for prayer, close your eyes, let go of what is around, and introduce your prayer word.

The third guideline. Inevitably thoughts will come. Whenever you become engaged with a thought, you gently return to your prayer word as a way of turning again to God. Suppose you are talking with a close friend and a noise from the street interrupts your conversation. You go to the window to look and find that the garbage truck has just come by and made a loud bang. Immediately you realize that your action has disrupted the good time you were sharing with your friend. You turn to your friend, apologize, and return to being together. In the same way you use the prayer word to say, "I want to return to being with you, God."

I like to hear symphony orchestras and will pay good money to attend a concert. But as the orchestra plays I can find myself deep in thought. Suddenly I realize I am missing the music, so I once again turn my attention to the concert. In Centering Prayer, when I realize I am being drawn into thinking about other matters, I return to my intention to be with God in that moment.

Or, it's like listening to a sermon. I have had an idea come to me as I hear the preacher in church, and in my mind I begin to pursue that thought. Soon I am aware that I have just missed several sentences of the sermon. I have to let go of the idea for now so I can follow the sermon. In Centering Prayer, as soon as I become engaged with a thought, I come back to my prayer, renewing my intention to consent to God's presence and action within.

Thoughts is an umbrella term for all the perceptions, feelings, images, memories, reflections, and commentaries that come to mind as we enter the calm of Centering Prayer. Thoughts will come. If they irritate us, they take us away from prayer. If we try to resist them, they gain a negative power that pulls us away from being centered in God. But if we let go of them by returning to our prayer word, we will continue our attitude of openness to God.

The only activity we initiate in Centering Prayer is our return to the sacred word. The rest is God's work in us. Centering Prayer, based in the theology of grace, is pure gift. In Centering Prayer we receive the gifts of the presence and transforming work of Christ. We do not have to repeat the prayer word continually. It is not a mantra on which we concentrate. At times the prayer word may become vague or disappear as we are drawn into our desire for God. Then we don't need to repeat the word. But as we become engaged with another thought, we return to the word.

Remember, we do not turn attention to the prayer word or center on it. Using the sacred word, we turn to God. The relationship is of prime importance. We turn to the indwelling Christ in Centering Prayer.

The fourth guideline. This guideline has to do with transition from the Centering Prayer period. You remain with eyes closed briefly before moving to other forms of prayer or activity. You might use these moments to offer some prayers of thanksgiving. You might slowly offer the Lord's

Prayer. You move from the quiet time to bring the interior silence that you have received into daily life.

The recommended time for centering is at least twenty minutes, which allows a person to enter fully into it and yet still fit it into a busy schedule.

PRAYER PRACTICE

Adopt a posture for prayer using the guidelines above. You pray with your body as well as your mind and heart. Your body becomes an expression of your prayer. Take twenty minutes for Centering Prayer.

Read again Jesus' teachings on prayer in the Sermon on the Mount, looking specifically at Matthew 6:5-8. What word connects for you? What teaching is especially applicable to you? Write it in your journal. Let prayer flow from your need as you develop your practice of prayer. How will you avoid "heaping up empty phrases"? Consider when is the best time of the day for you to pray. Are you getting up early to include a time for Centering Prayer, to listen to God through scripture and then to respond with verbal prayer? Bring a spiritual posture of letting go to be attentive to God into the rest of your day.

9   A Prophet's Insight

For God alone my soul waits in silence.

—Psalm 62:1, 5

Aiden Wilson Tozer (1897–1963), evangelical minister and writer, believed church trends were leading people away from a deep centering in God. For thirty years he served the Southside Alliance Church in Chicago. He wrote editorials and books that called Christians to a deeper life in the Spirit. Tozer saw religious people involved in "programs, methods, organizations and a world of nervous activities which occupy time and attention but can never satisfy the longing of the heart."[1]

Tozer observed that the rapid pace of modern life robbed people of the ability to draw inwardly close to God. In their self-confidence they were forgetting how to "be still" and know God. Tozer mourned the loss of the church's focus on a deep, intimate relationship with God. The church's emphasis on correct doctrine and teaching the scripture ignored humanity's basic desire for God. He thanked God for the few who "are athirst to taste for themselves the 'piercing sweetness' of the love of Christ."[2] He went on to say,

> It is not mere words that nourish the soul, but God['s very being], and unless and until the hearers find God in personal experience they are not the better for having heard the truth. The Bible is not an end in itself, but a means to bring [people] to an intimate and satisfying knowledge of God, that they may enter into Him, that they may delight in His Presence, may taste and know the inner sweetness of the very God . . . in the core and center of their hearts.[3]

Tozer believed that each person has within "a private sanctum where dwells the mysterious essence" of his or her being, a gift from I AM, the Creator.[4]

> From [humanity's] standpoint the most tragic loss suffered in the Fall was the vacating of this inner sanctum by the Spirit of God. . . . For so intimately private is the place that no creature can intrude; no one can enter but Christ, and He will enter only by

the invitation of faith. . . . By the operation of the Spirit "the divine nature" enters the deep-in core of the believer's heart and establishes residence there.[5]

Tozer's writing came out of his own prayer practice. He lay facedown on his study floor in silent, wordless worship of God, oblivious to his surroundings. He longed for others to find the deep communion with God that he experienced in those times of prayer. He said, "I want deliberately to encourage this mighty longing after God. . . . The stiff and wooden quality about our religious lives is a result of our lack of holy desire. . . . Acute desire must be present or there will be no manifestation of Christ to His people. He waits to be wanted."[6]

Tozer believed the spiritual classic *The Cloud of Unknowing* taught simplicity in approach to God by encouraging us to let go of everything by using one word that expresses our love of God. For whatever one may lose, "He [or she] will scarcely feel a sense of loss, for having the Source of all things he [or she] has in One all satisfaction, all pleasure, all delight."[7]

PRAYER PRACTICE

Sitting in your place of prayer, imagine that you are the size of your thumb and able to enter the vast interior of your soul. Go deep within and explore what is there. Be aware that you have entered a holy place, the dwelling of the Spirit of Christ. Stay there, and allow that entire space to fill with the love of God. Enter a twenty-minute time of silence, beginning with a prayer word that symbolizes your consent to God's presence and action within. Use the prayer word you have chosen, or follow the suggestion of the author of *The Cloud of Unknowing* by expressing your love for God with the word *love* or *God*. Disregard thoughts that come by returning to your prayer word. At the end of your Centering Prayer period, offer a prayer of thanksgiving.

Read Psalm 62, allowing a word or short phrase to speak to you. Write that word in your journal with today's date and scripture citation. Record your words of prayer in response to what God is saying to you. Remain in quiet for a few minutes with God and prepare to bring into daily life the inner calm you have been given.

10   Housecleaning

A new heart I will give you,
   and a new spirit I will put within you.

—Ezekiel 36:26

We may discover a lot of junk in the basements of our inner selves. Old wounds, past losses, and shameful deeds may lie covered, out of sight most of the time but still bothersome. A good housecleaning may be needed—not just the living room but the basement as well; not just tidying up a bit but getting rid of accumulated stuff.

Unrepented-of sin prevents us from welcoming Christ into the center of our being. Harmful attitudes and behaviors can obscure the grace of God for us. *Metanoia* in Greek, "repentance" in English, means a change of mind, a new mental state. We exchange the self-centered mind for the mind of Christ. We let go and receive divine forgiveness. We pray for the power of the Spirit to free us from harmful practices and attachments.

Clinging to attachments that have become dear to us deprives us of the freedom of loving and serving the Lord. Our attachments become idols that detract from our living in the grace of our Source and Sustainer. Fear, unresolved anger, selfish desires, false ambitions can keep us from God's desired fulfillment for us.

In a time of retreat I became cognizant of how much anger I held within. Numerous situations that annoyed me fueled a seething cauldron of anger inside. I knew I had to let go of it. But Jesus' words about cleaning house only to have more demons return gave me pause. I wondered what would take the place of all that anger. I invited the Spirit to come in and fill the space with love, joy, and peace. My prayer became, "Holy Spirit, grow love, joy, and peace in me." I took that prayer with me from the retreat and repeated it often.

Each of us tends to have a primary emotion that resides in us much of the time. It may be fear, anger, shame, or anxiety. Through the practice of contemplative prayer that emotion can lose its force.

My primary emotion is anger. Not that I am in a rage, but I tend to be a perfectionist, quick to notice the flaws in everything. So I am easily irritated. But as I allow the Spirit to transform me, I approach the frustrations of life with an inner calm. I can accept the imperfections that exist without being angry about them.

The same kind of transformation can take place for those whose primary emotion is fear or anxiety or shame. In Centering Prayer we go to a place of interior silence. Living out of that inner peace will greatly affect the way we react to people and events. A new attitude grows within us as we yield to the transforming work of Christ.

Holding on to bitterness, anger, resentment, or some other strong negative emotion blocks the flow of God's transforming love within us. When we forgive someone who has hurt us, we let go of resentment. We do not condone the wrong but adopt an attitude of compassion.

The prophet Ezekiel gave us this word from God: "You shall be clean from all your uncleannesses, and from all your idols I will cleanse you. A new heart I will give you, and a new spirit I will put within you" (Ezek. 36:25-26).

PRAYER PRACTICE

What is your heart condition? What do you find when you go inside? Lift to God what you find there. Take twenty minutes for Centering Prayer.

Read Ezekiel 36:25-28. Let a word from that passage speak to you. What primary emotion resides in you? What housecleaning do you need to do? Write it in your journal. Offer prayers of consent to God's desires for you, and bring that attitude of consent into your day.

11   OLD SELF/NEW SELF

Be renewed in the spirit of your minds.

—Ephesians 4:23

If I am full of my own self-importance, I have no room for Christ. If I am emptied of my ego, I am open to be filled with the new wine of the Spirit. Thomas Keating asserts that from early in life we have developed "emotional programs" aimed at getting the affection, power, and security we crave. Deprivation resulted in the development of the false-self system, which reinforced our desires for affection, control, and security when they were threatened. The programs we put in place seem to be the road to happiness, but they are not. We dismiss the false-self enterprise through repentance and receiving forgiveness. The true self emerges as we surrender the old self and its egocentric ways.

With self at the center, desires for esteem/affection, power/control, and security/survival take over. With Christ at the center we are free to be what God wants us to be. I always found it puzzling that Jesus said you must deny yourself (Matt. 10:38; Mark 8:34; Luke 9:23). I wondered how I could lose myself and yet have enough self-esteem and confidence to face the challenges of life. It helped me to distinguish between the false self and the true self. We deny the false self, affirm the true self. Paul said, "If anyone is in Christ, there is a new creation: everything old has passed away; see, everything has become new!" (2 Cor. 5:17). And in the letter to the Ephesians we read: "You were taught to put away your former way of life, your old self, corrupt and deluded by its lusts, and to be renewed in the spirit of your minds, and to clothe yourselves with the new self, created according to the likeness of God in true righteousness and holiness" (Eph. 4:22-24). Paul wrote to the Colossians that the new self "is being renewed in knowledge according to the image of its creator" (Col. 3:10). This new self is who we really are. We have a case of mistaken identity and work under the illusion that the old self is who we are. When we let go of that old, egotistic self, we can become our real selves, created in the image of God, the dwelling place of Christ, the temple of the Holy Spirit.

In 1 Corinthians 2:14-15 Paul distinguishes between the natural person and the spiritual person. Those living the natural life are the *psychikos*. They think and act according to external standards: rules, regulations, and customs of those in authority. They allow societal expectations to govern their lives.

In contrast, those who are spiritual are the *pneumatikos*. The Spirit of Christ guides them. They discern "all things," especially "the deep things of God" (NIV). They receive "the mind of Christ."

It is said that we spend the first half of our lives seeking to establish ourselves. We need to gain the recognition and respect of other people. Childhood and youth call for the development of the ego. Parents, teachers, churches, and culture guide us to become responsible, contributing members of society. In the second half of life we want to be who we really are rather than being shaped by the opinion of others. In life's second half—midlife and mature years—the ego diminishes and the greater self becomes central, finding our identity in God. Life becomes an expression of the inner life's moving into the outer world. Contemplative prayer is the vehicle for that inward and then outward journey.

PRAYER PRACTICE

Take some deep breaths. Slowly inhale, asking to be filled with the Spirit. Slowly, and as completely as possible, exhale and let go of every resistance, attachment, and anxiety that detracts from your love for God. Enter twenty minutes of silence with a word that symbolizes your intention to consent to God's presence and action. Turn loose every thought that could take you away from being open to God. Whenever a thought engages you, return to God with your prayer word. At the end of the twenty minutes, slowly offer the Lord's Prayer.

Read Ephesians 4:20–5:2. Stay with a word that grabs your attention. Listen to what God is saying to you through that word. What of your old self needs to be discarded? Consider the new self you need to put on. Write your reflections in your journal. Ask the Spirit to guide you as you take this prayer with you into everyday life.

12 AN OVERFLOWING CHALICE

I pray . . . that you may be filled with all the fullness of God.
—Ephesians 3:16, 19

I like to imagine that each of us is a beautiful chalice fashioned by God. As a chalice is filled, we can be filled to overflowing with the love of the triune God. To be filled with the Spirit, we must first be empty—a frightening prospect. We attempt to avoid the emptiness by filling our time with activity and our minds with information. We fill our appetites with pleasurable things, good food, sex, exciting recreation. We seek to possess, to consume, to control—all to fill the emptiness, and we allow our addictions and attachments to get out of control. Yet only one thing satisfies the longing of the soul, the one thing Jesus said was needful: God.

The accumulation of things does not bring us true joy. We live in a culture that esteems accumulation, but the math of spirituality involves subtraction rather than addition. The farther we travel on the spiritual journey the more we let go of possessions and selfish concerns. We relinquish ourselves to God until we reach complete surrender at the end of life on earth and enter into the eternal love of God.

Our possessions and attachments can fill the center that is God's dwelling place. A. W. Tozer wrote that in the depth of our hearts is "a shrine where none but God [is] worthy to come." He continues,

> Our woes began when God was forced out of [the] central shrine and things were allowed to enter. Within the human heart things have taken over. Men [and women] have now by nature no peace within their hearts, for God is crowned there no longer, but there in the moral dusk, stubborn and aggressive usurpers fight among themselves for first place on the throne.[1]

I've always thought of hunger as a negative. I find it unpleasant to be hungry. Yet hunger may lead to nourishment; spiritual hunger may lead to God. C. S. Lewis once said, "Our best havings are wantings." When empty we are open to divine grace and love. In his book *Addiction and Grace,* Gerald May calls our desire for God "our most precious treasure."[2]

Our Creator gives us this deep longing. In prayer, from that place of yearning, we open ourselves to receiving the gift of intimacy with God. Jesus said, "Blessed are the poor in spirit, for theirs is the kingdom of heaven" (Matt. 5:3). In our poverty we receive. Emptied, we can be filled with the "fullness of God" (Eph. 3:19).

Some people fear that when they enter silent prayer, the devil may come in. Actually we are protected when Christ fills our inner space. Martin Luther's hymn "A Mighty Fortress Is Our God" puts it this way: "Though this world, with devils filled, should threaten to undo us, we will not fear." The doom of the Prince of Darkness "is sure; one little word shall fell him." In the power of Christ, the evil one is dismissed.

In Centering Prayer one little word states our intention to go to the center of our being where Christ dwells. We allow the Spirit to transform us from within.

In an electric lightbulb there is a vacuum. The emptiness keeps the filament at the center free from encumbrance. Then, when electricity enters the bulb, the filament can burn brightly. At our center is the soul. Freed from egotistic encumbrances it can burn brightly with God's presence. Letting go of the desires of the false self frees us to let the transforming work of Christ take place in us. We will burn with love and faith, hope and joy as we receive the current of the Spirit.

Our Centering Prayer word expresses receptivity and repeats our intention to surrender to God's presence and action: We are open to receive the love of God. In Centering Prayer we don't constantly repeat a sacred word. We use our prayer word only when needed. Sometimes we need it a lot. Sometimes a moment of interior silence comes when even the prayer word is forgotten. In that moment we are most open to the loving presence of Christ. Then the chalice we are can become a vessel of blessing. Divine love and grace will not only fill us but overflow. The love and joy of Christ will spill over onto thirsty souls around us. "My cup overflows," says Psalm 23.

PRAYER PRACTICE

Stand with arms upraised and slightly curved so that you are in the form of a chalice. Let the Spirit of Christ fill you, entering every cell of your body. With each deep breath ask God to fill you. With each exhalation let go of the ego desires that take up space in you. Then sit in silence. Gently introduce your prayer word as a symbol of your intention to consent to God's presence and action within. Disregard thoughts that come to mind by returning to that prayer word as a way of turning again to God. After twenty minutes end the Centering Prayer period, and slowly offer the Lord's Prayer.

Read Ephesians 3:14-19. Take a word from the reading, allowing God to speak to you through that word. Write the word in your journal and reflect on what it means for you. What emptying has to take place in you for you to be completely open to God? What takes up space in you that keeps you from being filled with the fullness of God? Ask God to remove all barriers. Stay in silence for a couple of minutes before moving into your next activities. Take the insight you have received with you. Allow it to flow into your relationships and responsibilities.

13   SILENCE

> I have calmed and quieted my soul,
>   like a weaned child with its mother.
>
>   —Psalm 131:2

In silence, apart from the clamor and noise of activity, we attune our hearts to God. The triune God meets us in silence.

According to rabbinic legend, at Mount Sinai the people of Israel designated Moses as the one to listen to God. They felt convinced that they could not get close to God. An encounter with such awesome power and holiness would lead to death. As a result the people only heard the first letter of their alphabet. That is a silent letter unless it has a vowel attached. So the people received the gift of silence.

The Psalms encourage quiet, contemplative prayer. Psalm 62 says, "For God alone my soul waits in silence." Although there are those who will assail and batter, the psalmist finds hope in God. In silent waiting assurance comes. Psalm 46 says, "'Be still, and know that I am God!'" In the stillness we let go of all that would disturb. Psalm 131 says, "I have calmed and quieted my soul, like a weaned child with its mother." As the child rests in the loving arms of the parent, so we can rest in God's embrace. In this loving embrace we are held intimately. No words are needed. A weaned child is not demanding, simply fulfilled by being held in the mother's loving arms, receiving the gift of intimate communion.

To be like that child we need to be silent. I first learned to be free of the noise without and the clamor within by repeating the Jesus Prayer and biblical phrases. Then I discovered Centering Prayer. I first learned about it through books written by Basil Pennington and Thomas Keating. I listened to tapes about Centering Prayer recorded by Thomas Keating. Having a single word as the symbol of my consent to God's presence and action within helped me let go of thoughts in order simply to be with God in faith and love. This practice became part of my daily prayers.

In September 1996 I attended a workshop on Centering Prayer led by Therese Saulnier of the Contemplative Outreach network. That inspired me to add a second prayer time each day beyond my morning prayers.

This resolve was reinforced when I attended a workshop led by Basil Pennington. Since then I have included at least twenty minutes of Centering Prayer in my morning prayer time and another twenty-minute period for Centering Prayer later in the day. These times of silence, twenty minutes twice a day, have awakened my awareness of the indwelling presence and given me a greater consciousness of God in all of life.

In his classic *Of the Imitation of Christ*, Thomas à Kempis advocated finding a time to be alone and quiet for prayer:

Seek a convenient time (Eccles. 3:1) to yourself and meditate often upon God's lovingkindnesses. Forsake curious questionings, but read diligently matters which rather yield contrition to your heart than occupation to your head.

If you will withdraw yourself from speaking vainly and from gadding idly, as also from hearkening after new things and rumors, you shall find time enough and suitable for meditation on good things.

The greatest saints avoided, when they could, the society of men (Heb. 11:38), and did rather choose to live to God in secret. . . .

He therefore who intends to attain to the more inward and spiritual things of religion must with Jesus depart from the multitude (Matt. 5:1). . . .

If you desire to be truly contrite in heart, enter into your secret chamber and shut out the tumults of the world.

. . . In silence and in stillness a devout soul profits and learns the hidden things of the Scriptures. There he finds rivers of tears, wherein he may every night (Ps. 6:6) wash and cleanse himself, that he may be more familiar with his Creator.[1]

Contemplative prayer is resting silently in the loving arms of God. No words are needed to express this love. A mother may gently sing or speak to her baby, but she spends hours in silence simply holding the child who is content to be cradled in the mother's arms. At times hunger or irritation gets expressed in a cry. But for many hours there is a silent communication of trust and intimacy.

In Christian spirituality the word *contemplation* denotes quiet awareness of God. This consciousness goes deeper than words or thoughts can express, a quiet rest in God. *Contemplation* implies rapt attention to God, enfolded in God's loving embrace. *Meditation* in Christian tradition implies thinking about something, reflecting on its meaning. Contemplation expresses a deeper awareness beyond words, an intimate presence. We get a foretaste of heaven where we are "lost in wonder, love, and praise."

PRAYER PRACTICE

Imagine being held in the arms of the loving Creator. Let yourself feel the calm and security of being there. Take a word that expresses your desire to receive the love of God. Enter twenty minutes of silence. When thoughts come to mind, let go of them by returning to that word, which symbolizes your intention to be with God. At the end of the twenty minutes, offer a silent prayer of thanksgiving.

Read Psalm 131. Meditate on what God is saying to you. Imagine what it is like to be a weaned child held in the arms of a loving mother. Give thanks for the love of God, which is like that of a perfect parent. Write in your journal what you experience. Offer verbal prayers to God. Then give yourself a few minutes of quiet appreciation of the grace that goes with you as you move to other activities.

14 THE GIFT OF CONTEMPLATION

"There is need of only one thing."

—Luke 10:41

Contemplation takes us beyond thought and words into the mystery of the Trinity. In contemplative prayer we receive the gift of the loving presence of the One revealed in Jesus Christ. In contemplative living we go about ordinary life with a consciousness of God's presence in everything and everyone.

Our lives begin in a state of contemplation. From conception until we sense our separate existence as an infant, we are blissfully content. As this life ends we again yield ourselves to the Eternal One. As Jesus died he said, "Father, into your hands I commend my spirit"; so in our death, by the grace of Christ, we surrender to our loving God. We enter the ultimate state of contemplation. Meanwhile, between birth and death, contemplative prayer offers a means by which we now receive the gift of the loving presence of the Holy One.

We all experience moments of contemplation that are given to us when we are open and fully present. Contemplatives seek to live in that quality of presence more continually. Centering Prayer is a way of being open to the gift of contemplation. With a sacred word we open our hearts to the love of God. We let go of thoughts and let ourselves be in God and God in us. We wait in silence to receive the amazing gift. By divine grace we receive the peace, love, and joy of transforming union with God.

But so many thoughts come to us once we quiet down and rest: all kinds of perceptions, ideas, memories, reflections, and commentaries come to mind. We cannot stop them, but we can disregard them by using the prayer word we have chosen as a way of turning to God in faith and love.

So often we are "worried and distracted by many things." This was true for Martha. In her efforts to offer Jesus hospitality, she complains that her sister, Mary, is leaving her to do all the work. Mary sits at Jesus' feet. Reflecting his love for Martha, Jesus repeats her name twice, "Martha, Martha." Gently Jesus tells her that Mary has chosen what is most important. Martha assumes that she serves Jesus through her hostess duties. We also have responsibilities and serve Christ by fulfilling them. But one thing is most needed.

Will we sit at the feet of Jesus as Mary did? Will we be in prayer paying attention to Christ? Will we take the time simply to be with God in faith and love?

I always thought that activity afforded the way to serve God. In my activism I missed the contemplative dimension. I valued doing more than being, obedience more than a loving relationship. Like Martha I didn't think I had time for contemplation. Centering Prayer's discipline of regular prayer with a period of silence gave me a way to receive the divine presence. In Centering Prayer I sit at the feet of Jesus. I open my heart to receive the love of God.

We do not initiate contemplation. God always takes the initiative. We respond to God in Centering Prayer, saying, "I love you too." We use a word or symbol that expresses that love, giving our consent to the loving presence and healing action of God.

PRAYER PRACTICE

Imagine Mary's experience of sitting at the feet of Jesus. Enter her mood of attentive listening and adoration. Choose a word that expresses your intention to be fully present to the living Christ. In twenty minutes of silence let that word symbolize your consent to the presence and action of the Spirit of Christ in you. Let go of thoughts about other concerns. When you find yourself going off on a mental tangent, ever so gently return to your prayer word as a way of returning to the divine presence.

Read Luke 10:38-42. In your imagination be there at the home of Martha, Mary, and Lazarus. Observe both sisters and Jesus. Participate in the story in whatever way you feel led. Listen to Jesus' words to Martha and Mary, sensing how each felt at the moment. Be aware of how Jesus felt toward each of them. Then imagine that Jesus turns to you. Listen to what Jesus has to say to you. Write what happened for you. What have you learned about yourself and your relationship with Christ? Pray for grace and guidance, asking that you may establish the practice of prayer that will enable you to sit at the feet of Jesus. Give yourself time to let what you have received become part of you.

15 PRAYER IN THE EARLY CHURCH

"Jesus, Son of David, have mercy on me!"

—Luke 18:38

In the early years of church history some Christians fled to the desert because they believed that society was moving in the wrong direction. Instead of letting it sweep them along, they decided to live solitary lives in which they could give themselves completely to Christ. Anthony of Egypt, who spent years in the desert fighting demons and coming out purged and whole, inspired them. While desert living lessened society's influences, the fight against demons was no less real. The desert people armed themselves for spiritual warfare by using a phrase from scripture or the Jesus Prayer. Repeating their prayer sentence allowed them to dismiss the thoughts that lead to gluttony, lust, pride, and other sins.

John Cassian (360–ca. 435) visited these desert people and recorded his learnings in *The Conferences*. One of the oldest and most revered fathers of the desert, Abba Isaac, told Cassian how people of his acquaintance and those before them could enter communion with God. To release distracting thoughts, Abba Isaac would recall Psalm 70:1: "Be pleased, O God, to deliver me. O LORD, make haste to help me!"[1] Repeating these words, he let go of thoughts and turned to God, trusting in the Lord's saving power and love.

One of the desert fathers Evagrios the Solitary (also known as Evagrios Pontikos because he was born in Pontus in 345 or 346) spent the last sixteen years of his life in the Egyptian desert. He died in 399. During his desert time he sought to abandon the cares of the world and live a life of solitude. He taught an attitude of awe in prayer with inner watchfulness. This watchful vigilance guarded against thoughts that took one away from communion with God.[2] Evagrios warned against the devil's trickery of giving us thoughts that lead away from God. Even pleasant thoughts can deceive us. We may become focused on a feeling or thought instead of being with God in pure faith and love. All thoughts take us away from pure contemplation of God. We shed thoughts as our longing for God deepens.[3]

From the fifth century on, spiritual guides taught the use of the Jesus Prayer: "Lord Jesus Christ, Son of God, have mercy on me, a sinner." The Jesus Prayer comes from two scripture sources. One is the prayer of the tax collector in the Temple: "God, be merciful to me, a sinner!" (Luke 18:13). The other is the cry of the blind man by the road near Jericho who calls out to Jesus, "Jesus, Son of David, have mercy on me!" (Luke 18:38). A short form of the prayer is "Lord Jesus Christ, have mercy on me." The prayer's shortest form is simply the name Jesus. Especially in Eastern Christianity people have been taught to repeat this prayer constantly as a way of praying without ceasing. With the help of a teacher, people learn to coordinate the prayer with breathing so as to "inhale" the presence of Christ and to "exhale" all that keeps one from loving God.

Another desert father Hesychios wrote *On Watchfulness and Holiness* in the sixth or seventh century. He said that in prayer we give an inner attentiveness to God with the guarding of the heart from thoughts. Hesychios taught that one exercises this guard of the heart and inner stillness by repeating the name of Jesus. "Watchfulness" results from this ceaseless invocation: a stillness of the soul free from thoughts. Christ takes residence within us. Hesychios called this method of prayer spiritual warfare. He taught a precise sequence: first, enter the prayer with attentiveness to God; second, perceive a thought; third, invoke the name of Jesus and disperse the thought. This practice of letting go is brought into daily life by the ceaseless repetition of the Jesus Prayer.[4]

In learning this way of prayer, I began to realize how trained and acculturated I was in a reasoned approach to life. I had picked up a distrust of emotion and a strong faith in logic. But this repetitious form of prayer put me in touch with a deeper level than head knowledge. It connected me with my heart and intuition. The Jesus Prayer and other short sentence prayers helped me to be in silence and open to God.

PRAYER PRACTICE

Enter a time of prayer with the words of the Jesus Prayer. Inhaling, silently repeat the words, "Lord Jesus Christ," receiving the gift of Christ's presence. Exhaling, complete the Jesus Prayer with the words "have mercy on me," letting the forgiveness and grace of God remove all that keeps you from God. Take twenty minutes for silent prayer. Use the prayer word with which you have become familiar or the name Jesus. Whenever you realize you are thinking, gently return to that word.

Then turn to Luke 18:35-43. Read the story of the blind beggar by the road and his prayer to Jesus. Imagine the scene with its sights and smells. See the people, the road, the weather. Watch Jesus as he hears the man's plea and stops to welcome the blind man. Imagine you are there and Jesus turns to you and asks the same question he put to the blind beggar, "What do you want me to do for you?" Tell Jesus of the healing you need. Write your experience. Offer your requests. In a few more moments of quiet, prepare to bring an awareness of the healing Spirit of Christ into daily activity.

16   Centering Prayer in Christian History

> "Blessed are the pure in heart, for they will see God."
>
> —Matthew 5:8

Early in Christian history John Chrysostom (347–407), patriarch of Constantinople, taught prayer not made of words but rather of a longing for God too deep for words. Gregory the Great (540–604), theologian and pope, described contemplative prayer as resting in the knowledge and love of God.

Gregory of Sinai, a monk who lived in the middle of the fourteenth century, taught contemplative prayer as abiding in God, praying from the heart, and refraining from thought. This pure prayer is done in silence. Gregory advocated the use of the Jesus Prayer as a way of remaining patient in prayer and being free from wandering thoughts. Gregory said you cannot drive away thoughts, but God can. The thoughts will flee when you call on the Lord Jesus.[1] Also in the fourteenth century an English monk wrote a book of instruction on prayer called *The Cloud of Unknowing*. He instructed his disciple to "lift up your heart to God with a humble impulse of love."[2] We pray, he wrote, "in the love of Jesus."[3] We let go of intellectual ideas and imaginings to love God in "a cloud of unknowing."[4] We dismiss thoughts about things past, present, or future to a "cloud of forgetting" beneath us.[5]

> For a simple reaching out directly towards God is sufficient, without any other cause except himself. If you like, you can have this reaching out, wrapped up and enfolded in a single word. So as to have a better grasp of it, take just a little word, of one syllable rather than of two; for the shorter it is the better it is in agreement with this exercise of the spirit. Such a one is the word "God" or the word "love." . . . Fasten this word to your heart, so that whatever happens it will never go away. This word is to be your shield and your spear, whether you are riding in peace or in war. With this word you are to beat upon this cloud and this darkness above you. With this word you are to strike down every kind of thought under the cloud of forgetting; so that if any

thought should press upon you and ask you what you would have, answer it with no other word but with this one. . . . If you will hold fast to this purpose, you may be sure that the thought will not stay for very long.[6]

Through Christian history, this simple way of prayer has gone by different names. Teresa of Ávila called it the "prayer of quiet." Others have called it the "prayer of simple regard" or the "prayer of faith."

In the Middle Ages it was expected that everyone could engage in contemplative prayer. Then in the late fifteenth and early sixteenth centuries especially, many thought that only a few people could enjoy the gift of contemplative prayer. Common people were considered incapable of the practice. Most churches stopped teaching contemplative prayer to their members.

In the 1970s Eastern methods of meditation were attracting the interest of many young people in America. Three monks at Saint Joseph's Abbey in Spencer, Massachusetts, observed this phenomenon. They realized that this interest came out of hunger for a quiet and deep consciousness of the Ultimate Mystery. People were yearning for what the rich tradition of contemplative prayer in Christianity could provide, but most did not know about it. And the monks had no way to convey it like the carefully constructed methods of teaching developed for Eastern meditation such as Transcendental Meditation.

One of the monks William Meninger began to use the method from *The Cloud of Unknowing* as the basis for teaching contemplative prayer. He called it "the Prayer of the Cloud" and devised three simple guidelines to practice "the meditation" and to teach it to priests in the abbey retreat house. A year later another monk Basil Pennington offered retreats to major supervisors of religious orders. He quoted Thomas Merton as saying that we experience God by going to one's center and passing through it into the Center of God. Someone at a retreat said, "That's what you should call this method of prayer: "Centering Prayer." And the name stuck. Thomas Keating, the abbot at Saint Joseph's Abbey at the time, collaborated with Meninger and Pennington and developed his own statement of the guidelines for Centering Prayer. When he retired as abbot, he went to live at Saint Benedict's Monastery, Snowmass, Colorado. There he responded to requests to teach Centering Prayer. Encouraged by the enthusiastic response of people to the method, he called together people for an extended retreat. Out of that initial retreat came the desire to form a network of people that supported the practice and teaching of Centering Prayer. That network was formed in 1984 and now extends throughout the United States, Latin America, England, Europe, South Africa, the Philippines, India, and many other countries.

PRAYER PRACTICE

Begin your prayer time with thanksgiving for the gift of prayer. Be in silence for twenty minutes. Open your heart to God by using the word that symbolizes your intention to consent to God's presence and action within. When you become engaged with your thoughts, gently return to that word as a way of returning to your intention to be with God. Close the Centering Prayer time with the prayer Jesus taught.

Read Matthew 5:3-10. Let a word emerge that especially strikes you. Meditate on that word, asking what God is telling you. Let prayer grow out of that reflection. Write in your journal the date, the text, the word you received, and the prayers that flowed from it. Close by sinking into a contemplative attitude that will accompany you into your next activities.

17 THOUGHTS

> The peace of God . . . will guard your hearts.
>
> —Philippians 4:7

The wandering of the mind gives us difficulty when we seek silent communion with God. The many thoughts that come to mind are inevitable, integral, and normal. With the use of a prayer word we let them come and go. We don't resist or retain or react to thoughts but simply return to the sacred word. As we gain experience in the regular practice of Centering Prayer, we become less interested in the passing thoughts. The pauses between thoughts become longer. We appreciate the moments of peaceful silence that are given.

The author of *The Cloud of Unknowing* and other teachers of quiet prayer recognize that we are easily distracted from simply being present to God. Our minds, always active, quickly take off on tangents of memory or anticipation. We may become annoyed at the realization that we have been detoured by the thought, taken away from prayer. We need a gentle way of coming back to being with God. Instead of pondering the thought or reacting emotionally to it, we ever so gently return to the prayer word.

Oswald Chambers wrote a meditation on the problem of wandering thoughts in his book *My Utmost for His Highest*:

> After we have entered our secret place and have shut the door, the most difficult thing to do is to pray; we cannot get our minds into working order, and the first thing that conflicts is wandering thoughts. The great battle in private prayer is the overcoming of mental wool-gathering.
>
> . . . A secret silence means to shut the door deliberately on emotions and remember God.[1]

John Calvin's first rule of prayer was to be rid of thoughts that draw us away from God. We prepare our minds and hearts to enter conversation with God. We are invited into a wonderfully intimate relationship, "to unburden our cares into [God's] bosom." We need to find the way to deal with the common problem of being "distracted by wandering thoughts. . . . We are to rid ourselves of all alien and outside cares, by which the mind, itself a wanderer, is borne about hither and thither, drawn away from heaven, and pressed down to earth . . . but [instead] rise to a purity worthy of God."[2]

Calvin wrote that we are "freed from earthly cares and affections" when we are "moved by God's majesty."[3] The Holy Spirit moves us with profound awe and deep love. "The Spirit helps us in our weakness; for we do not know how to pray as we ought, but that very Spirit intercedes with sighs too deep for words" (Rom. 8:26). The Spirit guides our prayer and moves us into a loving relationship with God, beyond what words can express.

The Centering Prayer method provides a way of letting go of attractions and attachments that become obstacles in our prayer. With the use of a prayer word we let go of the thoughts with the intention of being open to the gift of communion with God: a helpful way to apply Calvin's first rule to be free of extraneous concerns in God's presence. As in Psalm 55:22: "Cast your burden on the LORD," and in 1 Peter 5:7: "Cast all your anxiety on him," so Paul exhorted the Philippians to bring requests to God "by prayer and supplication with thanksgiving." Calvin commented, "For we are not made of iron, so as to be unshaken by temptations. But our consolation, our relief, is to deposit, or (to speak more correctly) to unload into the bosom of God everything that harasses us."[4]

Unloading occurs in Centering Prayer as we let go of thoughts and return to the sacred word. They fade away when we do not pay attention to them. If a thought needs further consideration, it will return at another, more appropriate, time. Free from thinking, we enter a profound rest.

I don't go to the supermarket for the music, though some pleasant background music may come through the speaker system. I intend to shop, so I don't stop to listen to the music. The music may even annoy me when stores begin playing Christmas music in October. But I let that annoyance go in order to do my shopping. So with Centering Prayer, I let go of thoughts to appreciate the loving presence of God.

PRAYER PRACTICE

Do a bit of stretching before sitting down for prayer today. Stand with arms raised high and say in your mind, "Source of All" as you deeply inhale. Lower your arms horizontally to form a cross and say, "Eternal Word" as you exhale. Cross your arms over your chest and say to yourself, "Holy Spirit" as you inhale. Extend your arms forward and say, "Praise you, God," exhaling. Sit in an erect position. Give twenty minutes to Centering Prayer, letting go of thoughts to be in love with God.

Read Philippians 4:4-7. What word speaks to you? Write it, with the date and text, in your journal. Meditate on what the word you have received means for you. Pray for God's guidance. Bring your prayer practice to God. What are the Spirit's invitations to you for a regular discipline of prayer? How often do you take time for "supplication with thanksgiving" as well as Centering Prayer? Close with a quiet awareness of how "the Lord is near" and calls us to "rejoice in the Lord always."

18 PRAYER TOO DEEP FOR WORDS

> Looking up to heaven, he sighed.
>
> —Mark 7:34

Before healing the man who cannot hear or speak plainly, Jesus looks up to heaven, sighs, and then says, "Be opened" (Mark 7:34). With open ears and voice, the man can hear and speak. What happened when Jesus sighed? He looked up to heaven. So his sigh was prayer not articulated in words but in communication deeper than words with his heavenly Father. Mark tells us Jesus also sighed when the Pharisees came asking for a sign from heaven to test him. "He sighed deeply in his spirit" and then stated that no sign would be given "to this generation" (Mark 8:12). There is anguish in that sigh of Jesus, an inner anguish over the Pharisees' attitude. Wordless expression.

Paul employs the same word, which Mark used to describe Jesus' sigh before healing the mute man, to portray the groaning of creation and our yearning for God's restorative love (Rom. 8:22). He says we "groan inwardly while we wait for adoption, the redemption of our bodies" (Rom. 8:23). In this deep prayer the Spirit helps us. "We do not know how to pray as we ought, but that very Spirit intercedes with sighs too deep for words" (Rom. 8:26).

The Greek word *stenagmos*, translated as "sigh" or "groan," expresses difficulty in the power to act. We need God's help. We cannot reach God by our effort. In the silence of contemplation we yearn for God's loving presence and action.

In silent times of Centering Prayer, that longing grows in me. I don't want to miss those moments of the day. Not because I receive an emotional high, not for ecstatic experiences, but because the discipline keeps open my inner space for God. It is a time to sigh, to pause, to rest in God. It is a time to groan and express my deep yearning for God. And whether I know it or not at the time, the Spirit of Christ is at work within me.

In prayer we wait, said Howard Thurman. We wait for a "centering moment" that will reorient our lives.[1] We surrender to the presence and love of God.

In Christian tradition we refer to contemplative prayer as *apophatic*, meaning without words, images, or symbols. *Cataphatic* prayer uses language, symbols, and imagination to address and relate to God. We need cataphatic prayer, yet we know that God is greater than any construct we can imagine. In apophatic prayer we let go of all thoughts simply to be with God. We let the Spirit take us to a place "too deep for words."

In Centering Prayer we go below the cognitive level of language. Superficial awareness resides on the surface. Descending, we find a deeper consciousness. At the deepest level we surpass even consciousness, and the soul is completely united with God.

Prayer leads to loving union with the Holy One but not for private enjoyment. Prayer draws us into unity with Christ, into communion and community. Compassionate action results, growing out of the love of God. We receive the love of God and return that love in grateful devotion. We pray, not to get what we want from God but to consent to what God wants. Prayer expresses relationship, sometimes with words, sometimes deeper than words can express.

Florence Allshorn (1887–1950), a missionary and member of the lay community of St. Julian's in Sussex, said that the purpose of prayer is to know God. Our needs come second. More than asking God for what we want, prayer goes deeper than verbal conversation. At its deepest level it becomes communion with the triune God.

In his classic book on the power of intercessory prayer, *Prayer: The Mightiest Force in the World*, Frank C. Laubach writes, "The highest form of communion is not asking God for things for ourselves, but letting [God] flow down through us, out over the world—in endless benediction."[2] Laubach calls the effect of intense prayer a "loud silence."[3] Sincere and earnest silent prayer has a profound and powerful influence on people and events because God is at work through prayer.

Just as two people who fall in love have much to talk about, so we need to tell God all our trials and our desires. The couple spends hours talking and listening to each other. After they have learned to know each other through much talk and have come to trust each other through experiences shared, their relationship can become so intimate that they simply love to be together without words, simply enjoying each other's presence. Their intimacy may be conveyed in an embrace, which expresses their love for each other beyond words. Contemplative prayer moves into an embrace enjoyed with our divine Lover. So our prayer can become an intimate time with God, going beyond the words we say and deeper than the words we hear.

Especially for people who are more visually than verbally oriented, it may be that "a sacred gaze" will serve well. Imagine being in a dark room with your friend, whom you cannot see. Yet you sense your friend's presence and turn toward her or him. In Centering Prayer you turn your gaze toward God. That sacred gaze can be your symbol of consent to God instead of a sacred word.

The breath can also be a symbol of intention to consent to God's presence and action. Attention is not given to the breath, but the act of breathing can be a symbol of openness to God. In scripture *breath* and *Spirit* are the same word. Inhalation can symbolize receiving the Spirit. And exhaling can symbolize the letting go of thoughts. If breath becomes your sacred symbol, it is not a matter of focusing on breathing but on letting it be an expression of consent to God.

PRAYER PRACTICE

In a comfortable but erect position enter into a time of silence. Stay with your intention to be with God in that time by turning to your sacred word, gaze, or breath whenever you realize you are thinking about some perception, memory, reflection, or commentary. Close the twenty minutes by requesting that the ears of your heart be open to the word of God.

Read Romans 8:26-27. Let a word emerge and meditate on what it means for you. Ask the Holy Spirit to be the author of any prayer called forth from you. Be deeply attentive to the Spirit's movement in your heart, attuned to the prayer of the Spirit that is deeper than words. Listen for any soul stirring that comes from the Spirit's prompting. Record what you experience in your journal. Give thanks for the invisible, often unfelt, transforming work of the Spirit within.

19 THE SOUND OF SILENCE

A sound of sheer silence.

—1 Kings 19:12

Elijah cowers in a cave on the mountain where God has spoken to Moses and the people of Israel. Elijah comes there in great despair, shaking with fear. He had just experienced the greatest moments of his life. For years he has waited for a powerful display of the truth of the message God has given him. He knew his calling to be a prophet. He courageously spoke out against the corrupt religion of his time, a religion that included the worship of false gods. He preached repentance and asked the king to lead the people in the necessary steps. He warned of the dire consequences of disregarding God and God's will: drought, no crops—until there was a change of heart.

Elijah's stellar moment came as he confronted the prophets of the fertility god Baal. He challenged them to pray to their god to send fire upon an altar of sacrificial offerings. Pray as hard as they could, nothing happened. Then Elijah prayed to God; fire consumed the offerings, the water that had been poured on them, and the altar itself. This miraculous event dramatically demonstrated the power of the true God for all to see. Then Elijah prayed for rain and a cloud appeared, at first no bigger than a fist on the horizon. Then it spread over the sky, and the rains finally fell. As the dark clouds formed, Elijah ran seventeen miles to the capital city.

You would think that nothing could defeat a man who had witnessed such power. Yet a message from Queen Jezebel threw him into self-doubt and despair. The queen said Elijah would be dead by the next day. Filled with fear, he fled to the desert and fell exhausted under a broom tree. An angel ministered to him with food for a journey that would take him to the holy mountain of the covenant that God made with the Israelites.

Secluded in a cave on the side of the mountain, Elijah is prompted by God to go out of the cave because the Lord is to pass by. A rushing wind sends rocks down the cliffs. But the Lord is not in the wind. The mountain shakes from a rumbling, crunching earthquake, but the Holy One is not in the earthquake. Crackling, flashing fire appears, but God is not in the fire. After all that, as the New Revised Standard Version puts it, there comes "a sound of sheer silence." A sound of sheer silence.

"The still small voice," the utter quiet in which one becomes aware of the Eternal One. The words can also be translated "a sound of a gentle stillness"—a profound quiet more powerful than any sound, a quiet in which one senses the presence of the Holy One.

Elijah comes out of the cave, stands at its mouth, and listens to the word of God. Then come the directions that lead him back to his place of ministry. The word of God enlivens him. He gains an assurance that enables him to work boldly once again.

A depressed, stressed-out man. Nothing, not even the most powerful displays of nature impress him. Nothing can save him from his flight, his escape, his despair—except the still, quiet movement of the Spirit within, the gentle touch of the deepest chord within him by the mystery of eternity. Prayer without words. The longing within connects with the divine. The person with no faith in self is touched by the love of God. Fears disappear as the silence of God is experienced. Then the word of life is heard.

The prophetic word may be "whispered in the sound of silence," as Paul Simon and Art Garfunkel sang. Silence can speak eloquently: in the muffled cry of the poor, in the quiet movement of nature, in the profound act of prayer.

The story of Elijah tells us of a quiet voice to which we can listen. Not a sound that will vibrate our eardrums but a communication that will resonate in our souls.

PRAYER PRACTICE

Note the sounds you hear. Let them fade in your consciousness to enter a time of silence. With your symbol of consent to God, let go of thoughts to be aware of God's presence for twenty minutes of Centering Prayer.

Let the still small voice speak to you as you read 1 Kings 19:11-15. Let a word from that reading resonate within. Listen to the promptings of the Spirit that come to you. Pray for the strength and courage to follow those promptings. Write what you receive and your response in your journal. Take the interior silence you have experienced into your everyday activities.

20 FOUNTAIN OF RESTORATION

> My people have . . . forsaken me, the fountain of living water.
> —Jeremiah 2:13

The prophet Jeremiah invites us to drink at the fountain of living water. John Calvin imagined God to be like a fountain: the source of all, the Creator of life, and the one who provides for us daily. All the blessings we enjoy flow from the Trinity.

Jesus invites us to be refreshed by the water that springs up within us. As he talked to the woman at the well in Samaria he said, "Those who drink of the water that I will give them will never be thirsty" (John 4:14). Again Jesus invited people to drink of the water of the Spirit when he spoke at the Temple. Perhaps just at the moment when the priest lifted the water over the altar, Jesus called out, "Let anyone who is thirsty come to me" (John 7:37). The water of Christ truly quenches our soul thirst. And the water flows abundantly into parched souls. Jesus' hearers knew the prophecy that water would flow from the Temple out into the desert, giving life to barren ground. As we drink deeply of the Spirit of Christ, we flourish in love and service.

Jeremiah declared that, instead of drinking from the fountain of God, people had built cisterns. Confining the truth of God in law and ritual, they had captured stale reminders of God. Their cisterns were even cracked, said Jeremiah, so what they tried to contain leaked away. They needed to receive the fresh flowing streams of grace.

Prayer can be like descending into a deep well. Not content with a quick drink, we may become immersed in the pure, cool water of the depths of divine love. This can be profoundly gratifying. But it can also be frightening. Immersed, we are wholly absorbed in God. We lose sight of things that have been comforting. We lose touch with our normal securities and enter a place of pure faith and love.

Actually, divine light penetrates this place that seems so dark. We are bathed in the pure light of Christ. It seems dark because the brilliance blinds us, just as we cannot gaze directly at the sun without being blinded. In the deep darkness of total surrender, we are enlightened.

At times it seems that the well has run dry. Teresa of Ávila (1515–82), a nun of the Carmelite community in Spain, wanted her monastic community to adhere more strictly to Carmelite ideals. She inspired the formation of the Discalced (barefoot) Carmelites and founded seventeen convents. She is known as one of the great mystics and the first woman to be declared a "doctor of the church." Yet only after years of failure and difficulty in prayer did Christ come to her. Then she experienced his closeness, saw him, and felt his presence.

Teresa compared us to a garden intended to grow beautiful plants for the delight of God. Prayer waters the plants so they grow and produce blossoms and fruit. As we begin to practice prayer, it is like the laborious task of watering the garden bucket by bucket. Sometimes tediously, we daily attend to our thirst for refreshment from the fountain of living water, and growth begins.

Establishing a daily discipline of prayer is like installing a pump to supply the needed water. The garden comes alive. We grow in consciousness of God's presence. Consolations of peace and joy may be received. Some virtues form in our life, as buds grow in the garden. They come by the grace of God, bringing the delight of being closer to God than in the earlier effort of carrying water a bucket at a time. We do less and receive more from God.

Still better, Teresa said, an irrigation channel can water the garden. Not by carrying buckets of water or even operating a pump—with no effort on our part—the water flows. So, in this third level of prayer, God fills the soul with delight. Blossoms burst forth. The garden abounds with joyful praise and productive service. Fruit grows and matures by the grace of God. One enters both contemplation and active ministry.

A fourth and most wonderfully refreshing level of prayer comes directly from God, like torrents of rain or an artesian well bursting up from the ground. This water for the garden arises from the center of the soul, a fountain that flows from our very depths. This water from heaven saturates the whole garden. It comes when least expected and passes over quickly. No sensory experiences come with this level of prayer; it is beyond such. Teresa really has few words to describe it. It is a gift beyond human understanding.[1] "The soul that has experienced this prayer and this union is left with a very great tenderness, of such a kind that it would gladly become consumed, not with pain but in tears of joy."[2] God's will and our will unite. Fruit grows without our awareness. Joy blossoms.

> The benefits thus achieved remain in the soul for some time; having now a clear realization that the fruits of this prayer are not its own, it can start to share them and yet have no lack of them itself. . . . It begins to benefit its neighbours, and they become aware of this benefit because the flowers have now so powerful a fragrance.[3]

Grace and love flow freely, producing an abundant harvest.

PRAYER PRACTICE

Read Psalm 1. In your imagination go to your favorite place beside a body of water: a stream, a lake, the ocean. Let yourself sense the peace of calm water. Let yourself feel the cool, refreshing flow of the water. Draw near to God who is the fountain of all beauty, goodness, and truth. Come to Christ who fills the thirst of the soul. Take twenty minutes for silent communion with God using the guidelines of Centering Prayer.

Read Jeremiah 2:4-7, 13. Latch on to one word and listen to what God is saying to you through that word. Write it and your reflections in your journal. Ask God how you can drink from the fountain of living water rather than from a stagnant cistern. Be prepared to let your cup overflow in love for others. As you sit quietly, recall the beauty of flowers and of a lush garden. Give thanks for the rain and sun that make such beauty possible. What does it mean for you to be like a tree that bears fruit and provides shade? What role does prayer play in making that possible? Write in your journal what you are hearing. Give thanks for the gift of prayer that refreshes your soul. Bring the attitude of prayer into daily life so that the fruit of the Spirit will be produced.

21 THE LORD'S INNER CHAMBER

> You are God's temple.
>
> —1 Corinthians 3:16

Teresa of Ávila's bishop asked her to write about her understanding of prayer. In her explanation, she compares the soul to a castle.[1] The castle contains various rooms that lead to the inner sanctuary. People who never pray get no farther than the entrance. Those who pray occasionally get into a first-level room but see little of the light that comes from the inner sanctuary. Worldly things, possessions, and business affairs occupy them. As they let go of those attachments, they move on to other rooms.

So we enter the castle and at each new room we encounter resistance. The devil tries to keep us on the first level by breaking down our love for one another and destroying community.

We reach the second level as we persevere in prayer. Here we experience more attacks of the devil, which may cause us to give up hope. Vipers of earthly pleasures bite us. Our desire for esteem and fear of austere disciplines become obstacles. Yet the love of God in Christ sustains us.

By the grace of God we move on to the third level of rooms in the castle of the soul. The indwelling Christ brings us to a new place of security. We trust in the mercy of God, knowing that the merits of Christ secure our salvation.

Many, reaching this knowledge of salvation, move no further, never entering the inner rooms where the Lord of the castle dwells. Some become depressed, brood over their woes, and grieve over earthly matters. They cannot let go entirely; greed remains in them. They lack the courage and the humility needed to move on. Only with complete self-renunciation can one enter the remaining rooms.

Teresa advises that moving on to other levels requires assistance. A spiritual director can help us avoid the deceits and obstacles that get in our way. We can benefit from the wise counsel of someone who has gone through the difficulties and been to the inner rooms of encounter with the living God.

The fourth level of rooms in the castle is close to the chamber where the Lord of the castle dwells. Here we begin to touch the supernatural, which can be approached only with the help of the Holy Spirit. We receive "consolations" given to us similar to the joys we experience whenever something good happens to us. And there are spiritual "delights": gifts of God beyond what we naturally experience. We enter this fourth level by practicing the prayer of quiet. We surrender and allow God to work in our soul. This prayer is not of our doing but of our being. We totally resign to the will of God. Forgetting self, we have only God's honor and glory in view. Instead of thinking about God, we simply enjoy God's presence.

We must be careful, Teresa warns, to realize that this profound experience of God is only the beginning, just as an infant is nursed and not yet weaned. We do not stop at this point but continue the practice of the prayer of quiet. Satan will try very hard to lure us away. Sensible and faithful practice of the prayer will bring us to the next level.

Teresa calls the fifth level of the castle the prayer of simple union with God. No words can depict the remaining levels because they are beyond description. The mind cannot understand them. Few people find "this precious pearl."[2] In it we enjoy something of heaven on earth, this "hidden treasure."[3] The soul comes to life in union with God, which comes to us only by grace. With the death of self-love, we awake to love of God and neighbor. Our will conforms to God's. The soul that is so united with God has deep peace, yet at the same time sheds tears of sorrow over the state of the world and the lost people in it. It is not yet marriage but like a betrothal. By mutual consent we unite in love with Christ. The devil will try to break the engagement but cannot enter where the soul is united with Christ. We pray to be kept safe and intentional, moving forward to the sixth level.

Teresa calls the sixth level the prayer of intimate union. The soul is "determined to take no other spouse."[4] The longing of the soul for union with Christ deepens. Again we endure trials: the trial of criticism and being socially ostracized, the trial of praise, and the temptation to take credit ourselves. A trial may come through illness; there may be a time of depression. But the Beloved continues to call. The wounds suffered bring about a greater desire and longing. The flame of this love burns with great intensity. "So powerful is the effect of this upon the soul that it becomes consumed with desire, . . . so clearly conscious is it of the presence of its

God."[5] The soul will feel the heat but will not be destroyed by it. This "delectable pain" is an inner desire to wholly enjoy and love God. Delightful experiences may be given to the soul at this level: words and visions and rapture. The Beloved is clearly with the soul and calling it.[6] Teresa warns against coveting the enjoyment of these experiences but encourages us to desire only the will of God. Movement to the next level will mean leaving behind those experiences to enter a totally unselfish union with God in pure faith and love.

The seventh level of prayer Teresa calls "spiritual marriage." The soul "becomes enkindled and is illumined, as it were, by a cloud of the greatest brightness."[7] In this state the Trinity is revealed. "Here all three Persons communicate Themselves to the soul."[8] "The soul is always aware that it is experiencing this companionship."[9] "This secret union takes place in the deepest centre of the soul, which must be where God . . . dwells."[10] The appearance of the Lord in the center of the soul is not by a vision but by faith. The Lord reveals to the soul the "glory that is in Heaven."[11] In the innermost place of the soul we enter the most deeply intimate communion with God.

PRAYER PRACTICE

Offer a brief prayer asking that you may enter a deeply intimate communion with God. Give twenty minutes to Centering Prayer.

Read 1 Corinthians 3:16-17. What word from that reading speaks to you? What does it mean for you to be a temple of the Holy Spirit? What changes need to be made? If the soul is like a castle as Teresa envisioned, are you getting beyond the first rooms? Are you letting go of attractions that keep you from entering the inner sanctuary of God's presence? Write your reactions to the scripture and Teresa's analogy in your journal. Determine how you are making prayer part of your daily schedule so that you grow in surrender to the indwelling Presence.

22 GOD'S DWELLING AT THE CENTER

"My presence will go with you."

—Exodus 33:14

Liberated from Egypt, the Israelites come to Mount Sinai. Awesome displays of God meet them there. A thick cloud surrounds the mountain. Lightning flashes, and thunder echoes across the desert. At God's invitation, Moses dares to climb the mountain. There God gives Moses instructions, including plans for creating a tent to be erected at the center of the camp. It will represent God's dwelling in the midst of the people.

The people in the camp grow restless while Moses is on the mountain. Impatient, they create a golden calf to symbolize the gods that brought them out of Egypt. Their idolatry displeases God; God commands Moses to go down and destroy the golden calf. The people will be sent on their way with an angel to guide them, but God will not go with them. Alarmed, Moses pleads with God, saying they cannot go on without the divine presence. God relents and promises, "My presence will go with you, and I will give you rest" (Exod. 33:14).

With inspired creativity and sacrificial generosity the people erect the tabernacle at the center of the camp. When completed the cloud covers it "and the glory of the LORD filled the tabernacle." Even Moses cannot enter; the glory is so powerful. The word *kabowd*, translated "glory," literally means weight, heaviness, honor. An awesome and overwhelming presence camps in the midst of the people.

Divine presence dwells in our midst in Jesus Christ. "The Word became flesh and lived among us, and we have seen his glory, the glory as of a father's only son, full of grace and truth" (John 1:14). Christ lives at the center of our camp.

At one time Christian people organized their towns around a central cathedral or church. The sanctuary in the middle of the city indicated the belief that God is the center of life.

To be eccentric is to be off center. Eccentric circles have different centers. A person referred to as eccentric operates out of a different center than the majority. When self-centered we miss our true center. The living Christ, God's presence in human hearts, is our true center. God incarnate resides at the core of our being.

To navigate the storms of life we can switch to autopilot, yielding control to the Spirit who guides our thoughts, actions, and speech. We can pray that our intuition is tuned to the Spirit's prompting. Just as a person's conscience can be sensitive to what is morally right, so our intuition can be sensitive to the movements of the Spirit. It becomes the inner compass that points to the will of God.

Writing in 1916, Oswald Chambers talked about "discipling the intuitive light." He said, "When the Spirit of God is in us He gives us intuitive discernment, we know exactly what He wants."[1] "If the Holy Spirit is working in our hearts, ... we know intuitively whether we have or have not been identified with the death of Jesus, whether we have or have not given over our self-will to the holy will of God."[2]

At our center dwells the awesome, powerful, and loving Presence. Centered living flows from that center. As we consent in the Centering Prayer period to God's presence and action within, so in daily life we consent to the presence and action of God in the moment.

PRAYER PRACTICE

Imagine a command center at the core of your being that provides direction for all aspects of your life. That command center is not your ego but God Christ. The false self is removed from control; the true self, Christ in us, reigns. In twenty minutes of Centering Prayer give consent to that indwelling presence of God within you.

Read Exodus 33:12-14. Meditate on the hope this story gives. God desires to go with you. God's presence is your strength and compass. Pray that your intuition is sensitive to the Holy Spirit's leading. Write your reflections in your journal. Consider how the Presence goes with you throughout your day.

23 Our Mystical Union with Christ

> Christ is in you.
>
> —Romans 8:10

When we become truly centered, our lives revolve around God, not our selfishness. We are converted from self-centeredness to God-centeredness.

Christ dwells at the core of our being. Second Corinthians 6:16 says, "We are the temple of the living God." Calvin comments: "The only way God can dwell among us is by dwelling in each one of us. . . . Thus it does not mean simply that God is near us, as though He were in the air flying around us, but it means rather that He has His dwelling in our hearts."[1]

In his commentaries on scripture and his compendium of Christian theology, John Calvin teaches that we are united with Christ who dwells within us. Commenting on Romans 8:10, "Christ is in you," Calvin says, "By the Spirit He consecrates us as temples to Himself, so by the same Spirit He dwells in us."[2]

The writer of Ephesians prays for his readers in 3:17: "That Christ may dwell in your hearts." Calvin comments,

> Paul well defines those who are endowed with the spiritual power of God as those in whom Christ dwells. Also he points out that part which is the true seat of Christ, our hearts, to show that it is not enough for him to be on our tongues or flutter in our brains.
>
> . . . By faith we not only acknowledge that Christ suffered for us and rose from the dead for us, but we receive him, possessing and enjoying Him as He offers Himself to us. This should be noted carefully. Most consider fellowship with Christ and believing in Christ to be the same thing; but the fellowship which we have with Christ is the effect of faith. The substance of it is that Christ is not to be viewed from afar by faith but to be received by the embrace of our minds, so that He may dwell in us, and so it is that we are filled with the Spirit of God.[3]

In his classic statement of theology *Institutes of the Christian Religion,* Calvin wrote about our union with Christ:

> That joining together of Head and members, that indwelling of Christ in our hearts—in short, that mystical union—are accorded by us the highest degree of importance, so that Christ, having been made ours, makes us sharers with him in the gifts with which he has been endowed. We do not, therefore, contemplate him outside ourselves from afar in order that his righteousness may be imputed to us but because we put on Christ and are engrafted into his body—in short, because he deigns to make us one with him. . . . by faith we come empty to him to make room for his grace in order that he alone may fill us![4]

Our relationship with Christ is like the most intimate marriage. As two people become one in marriage, so we become one with Christ (Eph. 5:30-31).[5]

In this intimate relationship Christ "makes us, ingrafted into his body, participants not only in all his benefits but also in himself. . . . you are made a member of him, indeed one with him." Again, Calvin says, "Christ is not outside us but dwells within us. Not only does he cleave to us by an indivisible bond of fellowship, but with a wonderful communion, day by day, he grows more and more into one body with us, until he becomes completely one with us."[6]

In the Lord's Supper the Spirit of Christ unites us to him. Jesus told his disciples, "Do this in remembrance of me." Remembering, we "re-" (again) unite as a "member." The Spirit of Christ is the bond by which "we are joined in unity, and is like a channel through which all that Christ himself is and has is conveyed to us . . . the Spirit alone causes us to possess Christ completely and have him dwelling in us."[7]

PRAYER PRACTICE

Lift your hands in praise and thanksgiving. Know that the Christ of creation and redemption dwells within you. Sit erect and let your prayer word draw you into an awareness of God's indwelling presence. Give twenty minutes to Centering Prayer.

Read Romans 8:9-11. Let a word emerge that especially connects with you. Meditate on that word. Write your reflections on it. Consider your "mystical union with Christ" as the essence of salvation. Let prayer grow out of that meditation. Ponder how you can let "Christ dwell in you richly" throughout your daily activities.

24 Transformation from Within

> With the eyes of your heart enlightened, you may know what is the hope to which [God] has called you.
>
> —Ephesians 1:18

The prayer in Ephesians 1:17-19 asks that the eyes of the heart be enlightened. It is a prayer that the readers of the letter to the Ephesians will be given the insight needed to enter a life of hope, which becomes possible as we see God through the eyes of the heart. This enlightenment affects us through and through. The "knowing" is not just head knowledge; an intuitive sense of presence kindles the affections of our hearts.

Another prayer, Ephesians 3:14-21, asks for strength in the inner being. The prayer is that Christ may dwell in hearts that are rooted and grounded in love. In 1 Corinthians 2:11 and Romans 8:15-16, Paul states that in this center of our being we are in deep communion with the Spirit of God. Transformation from within will make our entire selves whole.

Protestant Christians speak of three aspects of the spiritual journey. The first is *justification*. Because of our fallen condition, sinful humans have to be reunited with God. Christ accomplished this reconciliation for us. He removes the barriers between God and us. We are justified "through faith in Jesus Christ" (Gal. 2:16). "It is no longer I who live, but it is Christ who lives in me. And the life I now live in the flesh I live by faith in the Son of God, who loved me and gave himself for me" (Gal. 2:20). We are fully accepted. Our relationship with God is secured.

The second aspect is *sanctification* through which we grow in dedication to God. "For this is the will of God, your sanctification," Paul wrote to the Thessalonians (1 Thess. 4:3). Paul then enumerated some specific ways we live a life pleasing to God: "control your own body in holiness and honor, not with lustful passion . . . that no one wrong or exploit" another (1 Thess. 4:4-6). Paul urges a life of holiness. What is set apart to the glory of God is called "sacred" or "holy" in scripture. We become sanctified, growing in holiness, by the work of the Spirit.

This results in our *glorification*. Glorified to give glory to God. Fulfilling the purpose for which we are created. Our complete glorification comes after death as we join saints and angels in the love and praise of heaven. As people loved by God we already live in that hope, "this mystery, which is Christ in you, the hope of glory" (Col. 1:27).

The classic way of contemplation also has three stages. First we need *purgation*. Sin gets in the way of a close relationship with God. Divine mercy purifies us. Christ removes our guilt and shame. In his strength we let go of harmful desires and allow love for God and neighbor to shape us. The power of the Holy Spirit makes us whole. The Spirit purges us of bitterness, resentment, grudges, fear, and hatred. In freedom we receive life with God.

Second, *illumination* shows us the way. By the grace of God our eyes open to the light of Christ. We see what God wants of us. We receive discernment of our calling to serve Christ. Being enlightened, we see our Creator's presence and work in the world. We are given vision to see the reign of God and how we can respond. Receiving the love of the Trinity, we find ways to share that love. We are guided in our walk with God.

Third, we come to *union* with God. We receive the embrace of divine love, fully appreciating God's love for us and being in love with God. In this relationship of love we are not absorbed into God so that the self is gone, but we are completely one with God. This union with our Creator and all creation fulfills the soul of each of us. In unity with God we receive eternal life, held always in the love of the Trinity.

PRAYER PRACTICE

As you prepare to enter Centering Prayer, let go of any expectations of what should happen in the prayer period. Come without an agenda, open to what you are given. Remember that the transforming action of the Spirit within is not readily apparent during the time of prayer. Evidence of it comes later. Your growth in faith and love is the result of God's work; your part is to be receptive to divine transformation. In twenty minutes of Centering Prayer let your prayer word be the symbol of your consent to God's presence and action in you.

Read Ephesians 1:17-19. Listen for the word God speaks to you. Write that word and your meditation on it in your journal. Pray that you may willingly receive the working of God in your life. Take that willingness into your activities.

25 Seeking the Face of God

> The glory of God in the face of Jesus Christ.
>
> —2 Corinthians 4:6

The Hebrew Scriptures speak almost four hundred times about the face of God. After his encounter at Peniel Jacob said, "I have seen God face to face" (Gen. 32:30). Psalm 27:8 says, "Your face, LORD, do I seek." God promises to Solomon in 2 Chronicles 7:14, "If my people who are called by my name humble themselves, pray, seek my face, and turn from their wicked ways, then I will hear from heaven, and will forgive their sin and heal their land." The promise is given in Revelation that in the future city of God we "will see his face" (22:4).

Paul anticipates the time when we will see face-to-face (1 Cor. 13:12)—not dimly as reflected in a mirror but directly. Not a distant relationship with God but intimate and close.

God gave information to Moses face-to-face. Exodus and Deuteronomy say they conversed intimately: *paniym el paniym* (Exod. 33:11; Deut. 34:10). In Numbers another word describes the close relationship between Moses and God, the word *peh*. God communicated with Moses *peh el peh*, "mouth to mouth" (12:8). God related to Moses, not through the visions and dreams often given to prophets but in intimate communion.

We prefer to communicate with people face-to-face rather than at a distance. We send and receive messages by e-mail. By talking on the telephone we have the benefit of hearing a person's voice. His or her tone can impart happiness or sadness. Only in face-to-face conversation do we gain the added benefit of seeing facial expressions. Body language tells us much about the mood and intention of the person.

I watched the construction of the World Trade Center, since I lived just across the Hudson River at the time. Everyone in the building could communicate electronically. The building was wired for conference calls to avoid the expense of bringing people together for meetings. However, people preferred to get together because they communicated more effectively when in the same room.

In our most vivid imagination we cannot fathom the greatness and majesty of the Holy One. Yet the Bible encourages our knowing God face-to-face. Jesus provides a human face by which we find God. Second Corinthians 4:6 says, "[God] has shone in our hearts to give the light of the knowledge of the glory of God in the face of Jesus Christ." By faith-inspired intuition we see God in all things. Our closeness to God permits us to see God's face. This intimate communion can be ours by the grace of God. The daily practice of prayer deepens that intimacy.

I'm convinced that at the core of our being we long to be united with God. Yet, at the same time, we fear meeting our Maker. So that which most strongly attracts also most frightens. Our thoughts about God can actually help us avoid intimacy with God by filling our quiet time with needs and wants. We can intellectually study scripture instead of drawing close to the Author.

We may feel unworthy to be close to God. Not fully accepting divine forgiveness, we feel excluded. We may think that only saints and mystics can have a close relationship with God.

Protestant reformers taught the idea of the priesthood of all believers, which encouraged everyone to be in a close relationship with God. In the movement of Pietism, individuals and prayer groups engaged in spontaneous prayer springing out of inward devotion. In the Roman Catholic Church, Ignatius of Loyola taught "Spiritual Exercises" by which actively engaged people could enter into contemplation. But fearing excess and heresy, church authorities often discouraged people from trying the contemplative dimensions of prayer.

Thank God for the current movement of renewed interest in contemplative prayer. Books, workshops, and retreats help us enter the contemplative dimension of the gospel. The works of mystics appear in bookstores. The teachings of contemplatives are being rediscovered. The invitation to intimacy with God is renewed.

PRAYER PRACTICE

Read Psalm 27:8, 14. Take twenty minutes for Centering Prayer.

Read 2 Corinthians 4:5-7. As one word strikes you, meditate on what you are given through that word. Write in your journal as the Spirit speaks to you. Reflect on your relationship with God. Is it face-to-face or do obstacles stand in the way of such intimacy? Offer prayer, seeking the closeness with God that you desire. Write in your journal. In closing moments of quiet, be thankful for the fact that God's yearning for you is greater than your yearning for God.

26 INTIMATE COMMUNION

"If you hear my voice and open the door, I will come in to you and eat with you, and you with me."

—Revelation 3:20

Teachers of prayer through the ages have given us some powerful pictures of intimate relationship with God. Bernard of Clairvaux lived in the twelfth century. With magnetic charm and warmhearted humanity, his preaching attracted many young men to monastic life. He reached out to warring rulers, bringing them to reconciliation. Cities were won over to Christ by his presence. He wrote about human response to God's love in books titled *On Grace and Free Choice* and *On Loving God*. The biblical image of love in the Song of Solomon fascinated him. He realized that the most intimate expression of human love points to the intimacy we can enjoy with God. Bernard commented on the verse, "I sought him whom my soul loves" from the Song of Solomon 3:1: "You would not seek him or love him unless you had first been sought and loved. . . . From this comes the zeal and ardor to seek him."[1] Being so loved by God the soul "now ventures to think of marriage. . . . When you see a soul leaving everything and clinging to the Word with all her will and desire, . . . so that she can say, 'For me to live is Christ, and to die is gain,' you know that the soul is the spouse and bride of the Word."[2]

Psalms express our love of God. Psalm 18:1 says, "I love you, O LORD." Psalm 116:1 exclaims, "I love the LORD." John Calvin said our prayer flows from "this sweetness of love."[3] He used the same word to describe this "sweetness" (*dulcedo*) as did Bernard. Calvin envisioned us all being drawn into God's "bosom."[4] We do not stand in a far-off place of alienation and call out to God across a great distance. God embraces us with loving arms. We can pour out our soul while held close to the heart of God.

Jesus' disciples noted the essential nature of prayer to Jesus' life. Luke tells us that one time, after Jesus finished praying, a disciple asked, "Lord, teach us to pray." Observing his intimate communion with the Father, his followers wanted to learn to pray in that same way. They already knew the traditional teachings on prayer. As faithful Jews they engaged in the customary three times of prayer daily. They recited blessings in the early morning, at three o'clock in the afternoon when the sacrifice was being offered in the Temple, and at night. These customary prayers used memorized words of address to God and added petitions. The disciples witnessed Jesus at prayer and the depth of his relationship with the Father. He spent early morning hours on the mountain. He prayed all night before choosing the twelve apostles. And he taught his disciples about prayer.

Jesus gave his disciples a model for speaking to God. In the Lord's Prayer he offered examples of petition for God's work in the world and for our basic needs.

Jesus told his disciples to prevail in prayer like the woman who repeatedly appealed to an unjust judge, like the man who had a visitor come at midnight. When the man had no bread to serve the visitor, he went to his friend and asked for bread. The friend refused since he was already in bed; but the man persisted in asking, and the friend got up to give him the bread he needed.

Jesus said that just as loving earthly fathers give good gifts to their children, so the heavenly Father will give us the Holy Spirit. In answer to our prayer we are given the gift of divine presence and power.

Jesus taught his disciples to spend time in private with their "Abba." In the Sermon on the Mount, he instructed them to make prayer a personal meeting with God—not praying in a conspicuous display of piety or with many words—but in a secret place. He taught that in solitude we can enter into intimate communion with God.

In his book *Of the Imitation of Christ*, Thomas à Kempis wrote, "Shut your door and call unto Jesus, your Beloved. Stay with Him in your closet; for you shall not find elsewhere so great peace."[5] Quoting Luke 17:21, "The kingdom of God is within you," à Kempis said we go inward to find the kingdom and the indwelling Christ. He wrote, "O faithful soul, make ready your heart for this Bridegroom, that He may vouchsafe to come and dwell within you! For thus saith He: 'If a man love me, he will keep my words . . . and we will come unto him, and make our abode with him' (John 14:23)."[6]

In Revelation 3:20 Christ makes an amazing proposal to the church in Laodicea. He offers it to you as well: "Listen! I am standing at the door, knocking; if you hear my voice and open the door, I will come in to you and eat with you, and you with me."

PRAYER PRACTICE

Read Psalm 117. Take twenty minutes for Centering Prayer.

Read Revelation 3:15-22. What is God saying to you through this passage? What does it mean for you to open the door to Christ? Write in your journal what you hear the Spirit saying. Pray for yourself and the church, asking for openness to the Spirit. Give thanks for the intimate communion available to you as you welcome the One who comes in to sit at table with you.

27   Prayer of the Heart

I give you thanks, O LORD, with my whole heart.

—Psalm 138:1

The purpose of prayer, according to John Calvin, is "that our hearts may be fired with a zealous and burning desire ever to seek, love, and serve [God]."[1] In prayer, Calvin wrote in his Catechism of 1538, "We descend into the innermost recesses of our hearts and from that place, not from the throat and tongue, call God. . . . True prayer ought to be nothing else but a pure affection of our heart."[2]

In prayer we come to God with "sincere affection of heart."[3] Calvin wrote, "Prayer itself is properly an emotion of the heart within, which is poured out and laid open before God, the searcher of hearts [(Cf. Rom. 8:27]."[4] From that place at the core of our being we express our love for God. We make the offering of ourselves as expressed in Calvin's seal of a hand holding a flaming heart and saying, "Unto you, Lord, I offer my heart, promptly and sincerely."

The Hebrew word for heart, *leb*, may refer to the organ in our body that pumps blood. But often it describes the inner self, the seat of sensation and emotion of a person; the core of his or her inner disposition, attitude, and motivation. We can be of a faint heart or of a courageous heart, a hard heart or an understanding heart, a proud heart or a grieving heart. We experience emotions and form intentions in this deep place.

In the New Testament the word for heart, *kardia*, does not usually refer to the physical organ in our chest but rather the inner self. From that place within, good and evil thoughts can arise. Jesus said the mouth speaks out of "the abundance of the heart" (Matt. 12:34).

In the early centuries of Christian history, some of the desert fathers developed a posture for prayer in which they set their eyes on that deep inner place by putting their heads down, with beard pressing tightly against their chest, eyes gazing through their navels to the place within, which they believed was the center of their being. The expression "navel gazing" comes from this practice. Today we might laugh at their contortions and use the words "navel gazing" to describe a useless effort. But those wise old men of the desert were on to something. God dwells at the center of our bodies, the seat of our emotions.

From the biblical perspective, a person thinks and feels from the center. Thoughts, insights, and imagination arise from the whole person. The mind, which provides our capacity for thought, functions as part of the whole not simply the brain. Nor do emotions arise only from the lower part of one's anatomy; rather, they are a function of head and heart.

We enter prayer with our whole being. When we talk to God we employ our thinking faculties. Good thinking may lead to good theology based on biblical study. As we listen to God, we give thought to what we hear. So, of course, we use our heads—and more. We love God with all our heart, soul, mind, and strength, our whole being. We pray with head and heart, our whole selves in communion with our Maker.

Simeon, called the New Theologian, was a prolific writer and teacher of prayer around the year 1000. He founded a monastery and also spent years in silent retreat. He warned against prayer that is only in the head. Instead, he said that the mind should be in the heart. We pray from the depths of the heart, enjoying the love of Christ.

As John Calvin reflected on Jesus' teachings, he wrote that we are to pray to our Father who is in secret: "By these words, as I understand them, he taught us to seek a retreat that would help us to descend into our heart with our whole thought and enter deeply within. He promises that God, whose temples our bodies ought to be, will be near to us in the affections of our hearts." [cf. II Cor. 6:16]."[5]

For John Calvin, to enter into the private room of prayer is to "descend into our heart with our whole thought and enter deeply within."[6] But many of us who consider ourselves spiritual descendants of Calvin prefer to stay in our heads. We trust our minds more than our hearts. We quote the verse that says, "The heart is deceitful above all things" (Jer. 17:9, NIV). But scripture also teaches us to approach God "with a true heart in full assurance of faith, with our hearts sprinkled clean [by the blood of Jesus]" (Heb. 10:22). The prayer in Ephesians is "that Christ may dwell in your hearts through faith" (3:17). From the heart, indwelt by Christ, our prayers arise. Psalm 138:1 says, "I give you thanks, O LORD, with my whole heart." From the heart, the center of our being, flows the love of God that we express in our prayers and our daily living.

In the nineteenth century, Russian mystic Theophan the Recluse spoke of prayer this way, "One must descend with the mind into the heart, and there stand before the face of the Lord, ever-present, all-seeing, within you."[7]

PRAYER PRACTICE

Stand with feet shoulder width apart. Lean as much as you can forward, backward, and side to side. Notice where your center of gravity is located as you keep your balance. It is somewhere near the center of your torso. That center is what the Bible calls the heart. Yet, it is located lower than the organ you call the heart that pumps blood. It is more in the region of the belly or intestines, where you experience your gut feelings. This is the center of your being. Spend twenty minutes in Centering Prayer, yielding that time to the indwelling Christ and his love for you.

Read Psalm 138. What word speaks to your heart? Write your heart's response to the word you receive. What does it mean for you to have Christ at the center? Bring to prayer the letting go of desire for affection, control, and security, which is necessary for Christ to live in you. Let the joy of Christ fill your heart, and may your heart rejoice in God's love.

28 PRAYER AS RECEPTIVITY

> By grace you have been saved through faith, and this is not
> your own doing; it is the gift of God.
>
> —Ephesians 2:8

In practicing Centering Prayer we rely totally on the grace of God and adopt a stance of receptivity. We do not concentrate or focus our attention; we do nothing except to let go of our thoughts and efforts and consent to God's presence and action. All else is the work of the divine. We simply open ourselves to receive the love of God, given to us by grace.

Other methods of prayer require concentration. Some forms of prayer involve passionate petition. In intercession we earnestly bring our concerns to God. In listening prayer we give rapt attention to what God is saying to us. Mantric meditation employs concentration. The constant repetition of the mantra or short phrase helps the pray-er focus and move into another state of consciousness. Concentration can make us more attentive. Mindfulness meditation can increase awareness.

Centering Prayer does not require constant use of a mantra or consciousness of breathing or any effort of exerted attention. Letting go of all our efforts, we simply sit with the intention of surrendering to God. We wait with openness, turning to God through the use of our prayer word that expresses our readiness to receive the love of God.

In the early spring we can "force" a forsythia branch to sprout its beautiful yellow leaves by bringing it in and giving it water and a warm place to grow. But we do not make the leaves come out. That early sign of spring comes as gift. With the discipline of prayer and the warmth of a sacred space, God's love blossoms in us as pure gift.

To learn Centering Prayer I had to unlearn the method of constant repetition of a phrase or word. For a while I had used the Jesus Prayer and other phrases in rhythm with my breath as a way of being quiet with God. In Centering Prayer I had to learn to let go of that kind of effort. I found myself using the words *try* and *trying*. And then I realized that effort is inimical to Centering Prayer. In Centering Prayer I surrender to God's action. I do not try to accomplish anything. As I learned the method of Centering Prayer, I became aware that my efforts to do it well were getting in the way. The harder I tried, the more effort I exerted rather than trusting in God's grace.

We may crave a certain feeling of peace or elevated emotion. We may anticipate receiving a particular experience. Yet in Centering Prayer we discard such expectations and exercise a minimum of human effort. We surrender, making no effort to achieve any specific emotion or sensory effect. We release any expectation of what should happen. Our salvation rests entirely in the grace of God.

Seeking to understand why we express consent every time we use our prayer word, someone asked me, "Why is it that I have to constantly give consent to God?" Indeed, all the gifts of life and healing come to us by God's initiative. We give consent because God honors our freedom to refuse or to be receptive. With our consent we open ourselves to the grace of God at work in us.

John Calvin's discussion of prayer in his *Institutes of the Christian Religion* comes in chapter 20 on "The Way We Receive the Grace of Christ." In receptivity, Calvin's second rule of prayer is that we sense our own insufficiency and pray with sincere desire and penitence.[1] (See his first rule on page 54.) Calvin's third rule is that we pray with humility, relying on the grace of God. We come with an attitude of submission, trusting in God's mercy.[2] The fourth rule is that we pray with confident hope.[3] Our confidence is in Christ, so we pray "'in the Spirit' with watchfulness and perseverance."[4]

Receptive prayer will change our lives! With sincere hearts, humility, and confident hope we watch for what God is doing, and we persevere in the love and power of Christ. We welcome what happens, receiving what God wants to do with us.

PRAYER PRACTICE

Lift your hands with palms open as you ask God for complete openness to the gift of the transforming love of Christ. Let your hands express your desire simply to receive the gift of God—not to grasp anything for yourself, not to push or pull but simply receive. Enter twenty minutes of Centering Prayer using your prayer word, a symbol of your intention to receive the loving presence and transforming work of the Spirit of God.

Read Ephesians 2:4-10. Notice one word from the text, and hear what it says to you. Listen to the word of God that is given to you. Meditate on what it means for you. Pay attention to the feelings it arouses within you. Write what you receive. Offer prayers of thanksgiving, and pray for guidance in responding to what you have received. In silence prepare yourself to go out with openness to receive the gifts of God that come to you each moment.

29 MOVING TO ANOTHER LEVEL

Walk in newness of life.

—Romans 6:4

Sometimes we "hit the wall" in our run toward God. Sometimes we stumble over a rough place in our journey. John of the Cross used the dark night as a metaphor for these down times. Though difficult, they can actually be a time of transition to a new level of prayer.

A Carmelite monk in Spain, John of the Cross (1542–91) shared with Teresa of Ávila the founding of the Discalced ("barefoot") Carmelites. His efforts to reform his community resulted in his being jailed for a time by his opponents. While a prisoner he wrote poetry about intimacy with God; then he wrote a prose explanation of his poems. From him we learn about the formidable transition from spoken to contemplative prayer.

We don't like to surrender the old, comfortable ways. We find it wrenchingly hard to let go of long-held concepts and images in order to enter the deep, inner quiet of contemplation. We let go—not because we want to but because of God's deep work in us. The Spirit brings us to a profound communion with God.

The transition can be a "dark" time in which God seems absent. In the dark night we feel empty, unable to reach God. We lose consolations that may have accompanied earlier stages of prayer for us. We need to keep on praying patiently. Talking with a spiritual director who can point out landmarks and pitfalls and who represents God's presence can be beneficial. We may want to escape into busyness or be tempted to reject the faith. We may feel enticed to give up, to become cynical, or to despair. Basically we need to remember that God will see us through; we need to "wait for the LORD," as the psalm says. The darkness becomes life-giving if we allow God to work in the depths of the soul for our transformation.

In the dark night, pride gives way to humility as we give up our false self; we let go of our greedy desires. John of the Cross says that the dark night comes in two phases, the sensual and the spiritual.

In the dark night of sense we lose attachment to pleasures of the senses, which brings a loosening of our attraction to situations, people, and things. The night of the spirit goes deeper. The soul is purged "and made ready for the union of love with God."[1] Even pleasures derived from spiritual exercises have to be given up. Whereas earlier in one's spiritual journey words and images produced strength and emotional gratification, the night undermines all of our own efforts, leading to total reliance on God's power and love. We enter "a contemplation that is dark and arid to the senses . . . secret and hidden from the very person that experiences it."[2] The soul is reduced to a state of emptiness, poverty, and abandonment, "left dry and empty and in darkness."[3]

Purged of self-interest we discover that this time of seeming abandonment leads to a pure faith, not self-seeking but completely centered in God. This deeper relationship with God does not come through intellectual reflection, visions or images, or spiritual experiences but through contemplation, a loving attentiveness. John of the Cross calls this night of contemplation "happy" because it leads to union with God in love. "Love alone, which burns at this time and makes its heart to long for the Beloved, is that which now moves and guides it, and makes it to soar upward to its God along the road of solitude, without its knowing how or in what manner."[4]

In the dark night we don't know if we are going deeper into God or falling away. Three signs indicate movement to a new level: from discursive to contemplative prayer. The first is that old ways of prayer leave us empty and dissatisfied. We discover ourselves wanting just to sit and be quiet with God, content to remain silent for a while. Old pleasures in prayer evaporate. Old ways of talking to God and meditating don't seem to be working for us. This dry and dark time is actually God drawing us more directly and immediately into divine union. This is a dryness and darkness not caused by sin but by the Spirit's transforming work in us.

The second sign of this transition is that we ache for God in the darkness. We long for God. The cause of dryness is not *lack* of desire. Our anxiety actually signals our desire to follow God's will, wherever that leads. We are being drawn into a new way of love.

The third sign is the powerlessness of our efforts. Knowing God through sensory imagination or mental reflection no longer satisfies us. Rather "by pure spirit" God begins to communicate with us "by an act of simple contemplation."[5] John of the Cross said storms will afflict the person who is moving to another level of prayer. It may be a storm of selfish and lustful desires, of impatience and anger with God. Dark clouds of confusion, uncertainty, and indecision may arise as the selfishness in us is being eradicated. We can only yield to the transforming work of God in us.

In his book *Living Flame of Love*, John warns us not to go backward but to follow the leading of the Spirit. He says we must know that "if the soul is seeking God, its Beloved is seeking it much more."[6] For, as we are drawn to contemplative prayer, God "is communing with the soul by means of loving and simple knowledge, the soul must likewise commune with Him by receiving with a loving and simple knowledge or awareness, so that knowledge may be united with knowledge and love with love."[7] In detachment from self-seeking pleasures, physical and spiritual, we enter the quiet communion of contemplative prayer. We can enter "the innermost chamber of the Spouse."[8] There, in emptiness and solitude we "wait upon God with loving and pure attentiveness."[9] The soul may not be conscious of making any progress "for God is bearing it in His arms." Progress is made because God is working in us.[10] All that is contrary to the love of God is discarded. With all the dampness of illusion dried out of us, we can become logs incandescent with the living flame of love.[11]

PRAYER PRACTICE

If you have a candle, light it as a sign of faith that the flame of God's love pierces your darkness. Spend twenty minutes in Centering Prayer.

Read Romans 6:3–11. What strikes you? What does it mean for you to die with Christ? What "darkness" and "death" have to occur for you so that whatever detracts from your love for God might lose its attraction? What has to be cleared away so that the flame of love can burn brightly? Write your answers. In what dark and dry times have you come to depend more completely on God? Recall a dark time in which you later discerned God at work. Write about what you learned. In quiet, prepare to take those lessons with you.

30 Living Out of the Center

Rejoice always, pray without ceasing.

—1 Thessalonians 5:16-17

The practice of Centering Prayer results in centered living. The transformed life grows out of the presence of Christ at the core of our being. As branches receive life from their roots, so the fruitful life comes from being united with Christ.

The best oranges grow on branches grafted to good roots. Grafted to Christ, our lives become fruitful. Jesus said those who abide in him and he in them are like the branches of a vine; they receive life from the Source and produce much fruit. As we live in Christ and Christ lives in us, we become obedient to his command to love one another. (See 1 John 3:23-24.) Because God first loved us, we love our brothers and sisters. (Read 1 John 4:19-21.)

Much happens when we take the time for Centering Prayer. Our prayer gives consent to the presence and interior work of the Spirit. We are unaware of this work in the periods of Centering Prayer, but its effects become evident in the rest of life. The fruit of Centering Prayer becomes manifest in daily living.

This attitude of consent becomes a way of life. It is said, "If Christ is your copilot, try changing seats." When we yield to Christ as captain, he transforms us from within. The old self dies; the new is born. We live in union with Christ and intuitively seek to follow Christ's leading.

Through silent prayer in solitude we become more keenly perceptive in the rest of life, more deeply conscious of the Creator and all creation. We become aware of God in every moment.

When centered we live from the inside out. Commonly we live the other way around. Governed by what others expect of us and controlled by our circumstances, we lack the freedom and the power to make our own decisions. Other people, our work, our attachments and addictions all conspire to keep us captive to their power. When we find our true selves we are free to live out of our true center.

The practice of using an active prayer can help us stay centered. An active prayer is a brief sentence prayer that expresses our intention to consent to God in each moment of daily living. The Hebrew people repeated phrases from the Psalms under their breath. The desert fathers of the third and fourth centuries taught unceasing prayer by repeating words of scripture. Repetition of the Jesus Prayer throughout the day can cultivate a constant awareness of Christ's grace.

Ron DelBene refers to active prayer as a "breath prayer."[1] Following his suggestions, I developed a short prayer that expresses my desire to bring a contemplative attitude to the day. I use this brief phrase at moments that do not require mental concentration, such as while standing in line at the post office, washing dishes, or jogging. Currently, my active prayer is "God, keep me aware of your presence."

This short sentence prayer may be called breath prayer because it can be said in one breath. And it keeps us in tune with the breath, the Spirit of God in every moment. As with the Jesus Prayer a person may use it with each inhalation and exhalation. It brings prayer into daily activities and heightens our awareness of God's presence in the moment. It becomes part of our subconscious awareness.

PRAYER PRACTICE

Read Psalm 70. Be in Centering Prayer for twenty minutes.

Read 1 Thessalonians 5:16-24. What is God saying to you through this text? How can you bring a prayerful attitude into the events of the day? Write in your journal.

Take a few minutes to form a "breath prayer." Ask the Holy Spirit to help you sense your deepest desire. Let a short sentence emerge from within that expresses that deep longing. Put with those words your favorite name for God. Take that prayer with you, recalling it whenever you have a reflective moment.

31 DAILY PRAYER

O God, you are my God, I seek you,
my soul thirsts for you.

—Psalm 63:1

In her book *When in Doubt Sing: Experiencing Prayer in Everyday Life*, Jane Redmont tells a story about the late Cardinal Joseph Bernardin of Chicago. "Years before he came to Chicago, Bernardin had 'a kind of conversion experience.'" Archbishop Bernardin was giving a day of reflection to "a handful of Cincinnati priests that he had ordained a few months earlier: a kind of 'touch-up' retreat for the new guys. In the midst of one conference on 'Practicalities of Prayer for the Diocesan Priest,' he told the young priests that, as a busy bishop, his pastoral responsibilities did not really allow him to sit down for a block of time, even fifteen minutes, and simply pray. 'What I learned to do is make my work my prayer,' he told the new priests." But their reaction surprised Bernardin: "Instead of taking in the wisdom of their bishop, three of them came up and told me they were flabbergasted. One told me he was scandalized. The three new priests didn't just offer a protest." Bernardin continued, "'They told me that they would support me in any way possible to start a habit of setting aside a significant block of time each day for personal prayer.' And they followed through. They came over and prayed with him. They sent notes of encouragement. They 'stayed on his case.'"

"It changed my life," Bernardin acknowledged. "It changed my priesthood; it changed my personal relation with Christ."

Bernardin set aside the first hour of his day for personal prayer. "Usually, that hour begins at five-thirty. But if I have to get an early start, I just have to get up a little earlier for what has become the most important hour of my day."[1]

John Calvin advocated that we pray constantly. He said we should lift our hearts to God at all times and pray without ceasing.[2] Yet, according to Calvin, we need, because of our weakness, to set certain hours for prayer: "These are: when we arise in the morning, before we begin daily work, when we sit down to a meal, when by God's blessing we have eaten, when we are getting ready to retire."[3] By spending the time at "certain hours" as Calvin recommended we come into a closer relationship with God. An awareness of God in every moment results.

John Calvin taught that we cannot pray effectively in public unless that prayer grows out of a private practice of personal prayer. He said,

> Prayer is . . . principally lodged in the heart and requires a tranquillity far from all our teeming cares. The Lord himself also, therefore, with good reason, when he determined to devote himself more intensely to prayers, habitually withdrew to a quiet spot far away from the tumult . . . ; but he did so to impress us with his example that we must not neglect these helps, whereby our mind, too unsteady by itself, more inclines to earnest application to prayer. . . . Again, he who neglects to pray alone and in private, however unremittingly he may frequent public assemblies, there contrives only windy prayers, for he defers more to the opinion of men than to the secret judgment of God.[4]

In 1907 George W. Noble published a booklet of prayers. In it he offered this sage advice concerning prayer:

> Take time to be separate from all friends and all duties, all cares and all joys; time to be still and quiet before God. Take time not only to secure stillness from man and the world, but from self and its energy. Let the Word and prayer be very precious, but remember even these may hinder the quiet waiting. The activity of the mind in studying the Word or giving expression to its thoughts in prayer, the activities of the heart, with its desires and hopes and fears, may so engage us that we do not come to the still waiting on the All Glorious One. Though at first it may appear difficult to know how thus quietly to wait, with the activities of the mind and heart for a time subdued, every effort after it will be rewarded. We shall find that it grows upon us, and the little season of silent worship will bring a peace and a rest that gives a blessing not only in prayer, but all the day.[5]

Practicing Centering Prayer twice a day for at least twenty minutes each time helps us in our daily walk with God. Once a day is needed for maintenance; twice a day leads to growth. Consider an early morning time and perhaps a late afternoon or an early evening time. The choice depends on schedule. Some do it in a lunch break. Some stop at a chapel on the way home. Some people practice late at night, but most of us are too tired by then. Each of us has to find the time that is our personal best.

PRAYER PRACTICE

If you have a symbol of God's presence in your place of prayer, take a moment to reflect on that symbol and on the divine presence it expresses. Take twenty minutes for Centering Prayer.

Read Psalm 63:1-8. What is being said to you about your daily practice of prayer? Write what you receive. What has a scheduled daily prayer time meant for you? How can you enhance your daily practice? Write the invitations of the Spirit that are given to you.

32 CONSOLATIONS

"I love you."

—John 21:17

If it seems that nothing is happening in your Centering Prayer time, that is good. In Centering Prayer we let go of thoughts, words, feelings, and emotional experiences.

To meet our need, God sometimes grants the gift of an emotionally moving experience. On a Centering Prayer retreat at the De Sales Center, Brooklyn, Michigan, in 2001, I was given an intense experience of the love of God, which filled me with elation and brought tears to my eyes. All I could do was gratefully receive it and let an intense love of God fill my whole being.

At the concluding service of the retreat, Father Ken McKenna gave a homily about Jesus asking Peter, "Do you love me?" Peter answers, "Yes, Lord." And Jesus responds, "Feed my sheep." That response seemed to confirm my call to help others enter a loving, intimate relationship with God through prayer. Remembering that experience encourages me. I needed that moment. God will give us the gifts we need.

Spending quiet time with God may bring wonderful consolations. At times in Centering Prayer, the love of God becomes tangibly felt. At other moments, a deep joy arises. Tears may fill our eyes because of emotions stirred within us. When consolations are given to us in Centering Prayer, we receive them with gratitude, not dwelling on them then but continuing with the intent of the prayer: to be with God.

People experience consolations in different ways and at different times. So we come to Centering Prayer without expectations. In Centering Prayer we receive the gift of a loving relationship with God, not necessarily pleasant feelings or any other reward. The awesome gift of divine love comes regardless of our emotional state. Sometimes we will find our emotions stirred; oftentimes they will not be.

Sometimes physical relaxation results. I may feel relief from a tight shoulder or a jumpy stomach after a period of Centering Prayer. The practice builds an inner reservoir of peace.

I thank God for times of deep joy and moments of intense awareness of God in prayer. But sometimes it seems that nothing is happening. There have been dry times. Then Centering Prayer has been like the laborious hauling of water from a well using a bucket. (See Day 20.) It became tedious and seemingly unproductive.

I had come to expect a feeling of inner peace that accompanied my Centering Prayer time, but then it disappeared shortly before a major transition in my life, my retirement. The dry time of no consolation continued throughout the leaving, moving, and readjusting to a new home.

I knew that the answer was not to abandon the prayer. As hard as it was, the discipline of praying twenty minutes twice a day was more needed now than ever. I did not know how to escape this drought. I remained in this desert for five months, during which time I learned some important lessons.

I learned these lessons by talking to trusted retreat leaders. (I had no spiritual director during this time because of the move.) I also found instructive a book by Thomas H. Green called *When the Well Runs Dry: Prayer beyond the Beginnings.* The book helped me realize that any consolations I receive come from God. Nothing I do produces them. If and when they come, it is only because God has chosen to give them.

I discovered that it is all right to be in darkness. I do not need emotional experiences in order to receive God's presence. God *is* present. My stance involves waiting, being open to receive divine grace whether I feel it or not. My love for God is purified when I receive nothing. Pure love expects nothing in return.

I appreciated Green's analogy of floating rather than swimming. I exert my effort to move in the water when I swim. I allow the water to buoy me up and the current to move me when I float. "Floating" we simply allow ourselves to be led and transformed by entering the flow of the Spirit in Centering Prayer.

After five months of receiving no consolations, in a moment of prayer I felt the sensation of a touch over my entire body. There came a stirring of joy within me. The drought was over. The words that came to me were, "This is Christ." Christ was indeed dwelling in me, as he had all along. It was a wonderfully reassuring moment.

I learned from that time of dryness that I can pray without consolations. If consolations come, I try not to cling to them. I realized that I should not become attached to any feeling or experience. Even the most pleasant experiences of God's grace are less than God. Only God merits our loving attachment. The method of Centering Prayer itself can become an attachment to avoid, since the method always serves our relationship with God.

Consolations can hijack Centering Prayer. A pleasurable feeling, a sense of peace, or even an experience of God can be an idol that distracts us from God. Centering Prayer expresses love of God for God's sake, not for self or for spiritual pleasure. In a time of dryness we can be more God-centered, less self-centered. We let go of emotions, feelings, and experiences. Maturing in Centering Prayer, we look for no feeling, no thought, no thing—only God.

When Mary Magdalene saw the risen Christ in the garden at the tomb she wanted to embrace him and cling to him. He forbade her from clinging to him. Instead he told her to go and tell the other disciples about his resurrection. Even the best vision of the risen Christ, even the most intimate encounter with God are not objects to which we cling. We do not become attached to them but rather offer ourselves in love and trust to God.

PRAYER PRACTICE

Take a moment to realize the depth of God's love for you—an infinite, unconditional love. Recall a time when you were most aware of that love, or gaze on the cross and see God's love poured out in the passion of Christ. Know that God loves you when you are least aware of it. Be in Centering Prayer for twenty minutes in the assurance of God's love, whether felt or not. Express your love for God every time you use your prayer word.

Read John 21:15-17. What word jumps out at you? Imagine yourself in a conversation with Jesus in which he asks you, "Do you love me more than anything?" How do you respond? Write your conversation in your journal. What does Jesus ask of you? Write it in your journal. Offer prayers of gratitude for the love of Christ and ask for guidance in how you are to express that love. In closing moments of quiet let the love of God fill your heart. Go forth with the desire to be transparent to that love.

33 PRESENCE

In your presence there is fullness of joy.

—Psalm 16:11

In the country school of my upbringing, the teacher took attendance at the beginning of each day. She called out each student's name. When she called my name I was expected to raise my hand and say "present." The number of students was so few that the teacher knew full well whether I was there or not. But I needed to declare my presence, affirm my readiness to be a student and to be attentive.

"Present," I say to God when I pray. Ready and receptive, I am alert to the amazing gift of God's presence.

In a teacher-parent conference, the teacher told my mother that I was a daydreamer. I would spend a lot of time in my mind spinning imaginary adventures. I was often doing this when the teacher preferred that I do math problems or read a lesson.

When fully present I am not away in a daydream. Rather, I am keenly aware of what is happening at the moment.

When in prayer I am present to God. As attentiveness to God grows in prayer, the divine presence becomes real in the rest of life. I become aware of God in every moment, in all I see, in everyone I meet.

On a beautiful morning in northern Illinois, my wife and I were visiting the village where she grew up. Jogging on a country road, I noticed that the ripening beanfields and cornfields had a golden cast to them. I gazed at God's handiwork, impressed by rolling hills and blue sky. I also saw signs of the modern age and its inventions. Two columns of vapor ascended from the towers of a nuclear power plant. The tallest bits of architecture on the horizon were not church steeples or silos or grain elevators but communication towers for cellular telephones. I wondered, *Do I see God in these human constructions as well as the golden fields?* The nuclear towers seemed ominous. Could some terrorist destroy their protective shell and spill radiation over the countryside? We never live without danger, yet God is always at work. The people of the area benefit from the energy produced by that power plant. The cell phone towers speak of the desire for connection. They facilitate communication between people. The hills and the towers express love of God and neighbor. The signs of God's presence surrounded me.

Seeing majestic mountains and pounding surf has always given me a sense of awe. The practice of Centering Prayer has helped me grow in a sense of God's presence in ordinary things as well. I see God's creativity in a mundane object such as a brick in my fireplace. God made the clay from which it was made. God gave knowledge and skill to the people who fashioned the kiln in which it was baked. The energy of the masons who laid the brick came from God. I see the Spirit's work when I look at a brick.

God acts in every event. The force of evil can intrude, but in love God never fails to be present and active.

In one of the darkest hours of my life, God was there. At about 3:00 AM I woke from sleep. The day before, my wife and I had received the news that she had ovarian cancer. In her room as the anesthesia wore off, we were informed of this devastating diagnosis. Her first words to me were, "I'm so sorry." It was as though she felt she needed to apologize for having this happen to her and the prospect of suffering that it promised to bring. We were frightened.

When I awoke in the wee hours of the night, I got on my knees by the bed and I asked God, "Where are you in this?" And three answers were given to me. The first: "I am in your love for your wife," surprised me. In my concern and care for my wife, God was present.

The second answer: God was in the people who came to bring us comfort. The first person who appeared in the hospital room after we got the news was a pastor who, as a boy, had been in a church where I was his minister. Now he came to minister to us. I have no idea how he knew so quickly that we needed his visit. But he came and prayed with us. A church executive came soon after. A nurse, a member of our church, brought her love. We felt God's presence in these caring people.

The third answer: God is present in the suffering of Jesus. The image of the cross came to my mind. I received assurance that, as Jesus died for us, his suffering signals God's presence with us in our sufferings. God cares about our distress and loves us.

Recently our family suffered the tragic loss of a family member. My son-in-law died unexpectedly. The circumstances of his death brought to my mind the question so many ask, Why? Why didn't God intervene to prevent what happened? In my grief and anger I felt abandoned by God. Plowing through the many tasks to help my daughter, I found myself losing my focus on God and trying to do all things necessary in my own strength. Only my practice of Centering Prayer kept bitterness and resentment at bay, reminding me of God's presence with me and our family in the midst of pain and grief. With that awareness I witnessed numerous acts of kindness and felt many manifestations of love and concern in which God was clearly present. The reality of God's love and grace upheld me, and I was able to support and encourage others.

PRAYER PRACTICE

Recall an experience when you were aware of God's presence. Remember how it felt to know that God was with you. Let twenty minutes of Centering Prayer be a time in which you are aware of God's presence and in which you are—in letting go of thoughts—present to God.

Read Psalm 16. Let a word touch your heart. Reflect on what is being said to you through that word. Write your reflections in your journal. What have you learned from hard times? God's presence is never missing, but our being present is sometimes doubtful. What will it mean for you to be present to God in this day?

34 The Gift of the Present Moment

"Now . . . choose this day whom you will serve."
—Joshua 24:15

The great composer Pyotr Tchaikovsky once said that he had spent his life "regretting the past and hoping for the future, never being satisfied with the present."[1] How sad.

The practice of Centering Prayer helps us develop a great appreciation for the present. We become aware of the divine presence in the moment. Disregarding thoughts of the past or of the future, we live fully now. When thoughts of a past event come to mind, we gently return to our prayer word and consent to the presence of God in the moment. When thoughts regarding a future possibility come to mind, we gently return to our prayer word and awareness of God in the moment. Then we take our attention to the present into each moment of the day.

A bit of doggerel says, "Yesterday is history; tomorrow is mystery; today is the gift of God. That's why it is called the present." I like that. A book titled *The Sacrament of the Present Moment* has helped me realize the gift of the present. It is Kitty Muggeridge's translation of talks by Jean-Pierre de Caussade, a French Jesuit priest who lived from 1675 to 1751. De Caussade taught a way of living in surrender to God "so we leave God to act in everything, reserving for ourselves only love and obedience to the present moment."[2]

I thank God for the wonder of living in the present. For a long time I had been missing this blessing entirely. I disregarded the present, living in the past or the future. I rehearsed a past event, thinking about what I might have said or said better. I reflected on how I might have taken different action. More often my mind was already in the future. Anxious about the next item on my agenda, I was thinking about my next sermon, planning for an event, getting ready for a meeting. I expended a lot of energy in anticipation of future situations while missing completely the wonder of the present moment. It was like looking at a book: the left-hand page was past; the right-hand page was next, and there was nothing in between. Now I realize that the present is really all we have. The past is past; the future has not yet arrived. The present is where we live, where God is, and the only place we can experience the joy of life. This realization and the practice of Centering Prayer have helped me to be joyfully aware of the gifts of God that come so abundantly right *now*!

In the present moment I am in contact with eternity. God is timeless. God lives in an eternal now. I am a creature of time. It is now that I am receiving the loving presence of the Eternal One.

Now is the time to listen to God: "O that today you would listen to his voice!" (Ps. 95:7). The letter to the Hebrews quotes that verse, stressing that now is the decisive moment to be a partner with Christ (Heb. 3:7-15). Joshua called the people to decide whom they would serve. "Now," he said, "revere the LORD." "Now . . . choose this day whom you will serve" (24:14-15). Stop worrying about the future, Jesus said. Be engaged in the present: "Do not worry about tomorrow, for tomorrow will bring worries of its own. Today's trouble is enough for today" (Matt. 6:34). We are fully alive when we attend to the present moment.

My grandson John, who was three years old, wanted things to happen soon. He did not like to wait. One hot summer's morning my wife and I were visiting at his home. He asked what we would do that day. We had some places in mind that we might visit but had not yet decided what to do. John's mother replied, "Well, we'll see what the day brings."

We took John to a playground and attended a noon organ concert. We returned home by midafternoon. Late in the afternoon John came to his mother as she sat in the living room and asked, "Did we see what the day brings?"

With attentiveness to the present we see what God brings each day.

PRAYER PRACTICE

Compose a "weather report" on what it is like inside yourself just now. Bring that report to prayer. Allow the Spirit to bring about any change that may be warranted. Be aware that God is present here and now. In that awareness offer to God twenty minutes of Centering Prayer.

Read Jesus' teaching about letting go of worries and awareness of the reign of God today in Matthew 6:25-34. What strikes you in this teaching? What does this mean for you? Describe in your journal how it applies to you. Pray that Christ may transform your attitudes. Live this day fully, taking with you an awareness of the present moment.

35 THE MOUNTAIN IS OUT

"Though I was blind, now I see."

—John 9:25

One summer my wife, Donna, and I visited a cousin and her husband in Gig Harbor, Washington. We stayed overnight with them. In the morning we expressed a desire to drive to Mount Rainier, which was visible from our cousin's kitchen window on this clear morning. Often cloudy in that region, many days the mountain is not seen. My cousin encouraged us in our plans for the day. She looked out the window and said, "Today the mountain is out."

The mountain is always there, of course, but fog can obscure the view. God's loving presence is always there; God is not absent. The triune God is always with us and at work in every moment. But the fog of anxiety and attachment obscures our view.

With the eyes of contemplation we see God in all things. Isaiah 44:18 speaks of the blindness in which we cannot see the presence of God, "They do not know, nor do they comprehend; for their eyes are shut, so that they cannot see." The Gospel of John declares that the true light that enlightens everyone has come into the world (1:9). And Jesus said the pure in heart are blessed; "they will see God" (Matt. 5:8).

Macarius of Egypt, born around the year 300, said that wherever we seek the Holy One we find God. God is everywhere—above, beneath, and in us. George Herbert (1593–1633) wrote,

"TEACH me, my God and King,
  In all things Thee to see."[1]

Artists, with their extraordinary perception, can help us see God in all things by drawing our attention to the moment, the moment of deep awareness. Rembrandt was especially conscious of spiritual sight as his physical sight failed him. In one of his paintings he captured the moment the woman at the well learned about the living water that Jesus gives. In another painting he portrayed the moment that the disciples in Emmaus realize their guest is Christ. A waiter standing nearby does not recognize who he is. In one of his unfinished paintings from the end of his life, Rembrandt portrays the father as physically blind, yet "seeing" the wonder of his prodigal son's return. The painting on Rembrandt's easel when he died portrayed Simeon, with eyes closed, holding the baby Jesus and saying, "My eyes have seen your salvation."

One of the fruits of Centering Prayer is clearer perception: seeing God's presence in the people and situations we encounter. We begin to see with the eyes of God, which makes all images sharper. We see the goodness and activity of God with greater clarity.

The formula for baptism at Church of the Servant in Grand Rapids, Michigan, is "I baptize you in the name of the Father, and of the Son and of the Holy Spirit. And may you always know God's presence."

The loving presence of our Maker, Redeemer, and Guide is an amazing gift. Oswald Chambers spoke of this gift:

> The reality of God's presence is not dependent on any place, but only dependent upon the determination to set the Lord always before us. Our problems come when we refuse to bank on the reality of [divine] presence. The experience the Psalmist speaks of—'Therefore will we not fear, though . . .' will be ours when once we are based on Reality, not the consciousness of God's presence but the reality of it—Why, [God] has been here all the time![2]

I know that too often I am a practical atheist. If you asked me whether I believe in God, I would respond verbally that I do. But I may be living as an independent operator, acting on my own, running ahead or lagging behind, not in pace with Christ. I have lost consciousness of God in the moment even though God is actually there. The pace of modern living encourages me to adopt this attitude. Then I need to be reminded by scripture and through prayer that I would not even exist if it were not for God and would be unable to do anything without God's gifts to me. When I am spiritually awakened and see the reality of God, I reenter the world as it really is, and the reign of God in all of life becomes evident to me again.

I find it helpful to ask at the end of each day "Where did I see Christ today?" and "Where was I oblivious to his presence?" These questions sharpen my spiritual eyes.

When I see an event I am a "witness" of it. First I observe and then I testify to what I have seen. I am a witness of Christ when I see him and his work.

As we bear witness, people can see Christ in us. It was said of the first disciples that people could tell that they had been with Jesus. As Christ's work of transformation takes place in us, people will notice. In the amazing grace of God, our ordinary lives can become transparent to the love, joy, and peace of God. This witness begins with our seeing the mountain of God's grace and glory.

PRAYER PRACTICE

Recall a person who has been especially transparent to the love, joy, and peace of God for you. How has the grace of God been evident in that person? Give thanks for the inspiration you received. Take twenty minutes to be in Centering Prayer.

Read John 9:6-7, 35-39. Let a word speak to you. Let feelings arise and other words form around that word. What is God saying to you? Write in your journal. Offer prayers of thanksgiving for what you have received. Ask for perception to see God in every event of the day and in every person you meet. Ask for the strength and courage to be transparent to the love of God.

36 RE-PRESENTING CHRIST

It is no longer I who live, but it is Christ who lives in me.
—Galatians 2:20

As I am fully present to God, I become the kind of person who is wholly present to others. I can give no greater gift. When I am present I am considerate, giving undivided attention to the person's words and feelings at the moment. People deeply need this gift of being appreciated and attended, especially in times of distress. The first task of ministry is to be present to people in their need.

By being present to God for one or two periods of prayer each day, you grow in the capacity to be present at other moments of the day. When that presence flows from the deep center of divine indwelling, you become a beneficial presence to others. Jesus said, "Where two or three are gathered in my name, I am there among them." As we meet another, Christ is present. As we converse with people, we meet Christ. In befriending others, we re-present Christ.

We are, by the grace of God, equipped to be in a ministry of presence. Each of us has a personality that to some degree influences the other people we contact. When we can bring a loving and encouraging presence we bring a blessing to others. We can also speak helpful words, but of greatest importance is the simple act of being present.

When we meet with someone our awareness of that person extends well beyond the meeting time. The more time we spend together the longer that effect lasts and the more intense it is. When the person has shared the profound movement of the Spirit in her or his life, we feel deeply moved and carry the inspiration received for some time. When the person has shared a keen grief, we feel grieved and carry that grief for quite a while. Each of us similarly influences others.

What do we do when we hurt in empathy for another? Another person's troubles may disturb us as sympathetic listeners. We feel grief because of love for the one in pain. In prayer we bring our concerns to God. Our prayer may consist of two parts. First, we may hold the concern before God, waiting with it for whatever word or realization may be given. Perhaps an action we can take will present itself. Second, we let go and give the concerns over to God. The Spirit can enter the heart of the other and bring comfort and guidance. The painful concern is actually a gift both for us and, through our sympathy, for the other person.

Many churches are filled with anxiety. A conflict may have developed or some members may have become dissatisfied for some reason. We know from systems theory how discontent can affect the whole social system. Paul David Lawson has addressed this problem and the help Centering Prayer can offer. Those who practice Centering Prayer are less reactive and therefore able to generate a calming presence, bringing a nonanxious presence to an anxiety-filled system. Lawson says when members of the congregation practice Centering Prayer, the whole system becomes less reactive.[1]

Entering daily into times of silence, we receive the gift of inner silence. Jesus promised, "Peace I leave with you; my peace I give to you. . . . Do not let your hearts be troubled, and do not let them be afraid" (John 14:27). One of the fruits of the Spirit is peace.

Even in retirement I find myself busy with many tasks, and I feel frazzled trying to get them all done. I need times of quiet. Taking the time to be silent twice a day cultivates inner peace. It builds a reservoir of inner calm. I can take that reservoir with me into daily life. As I meet up with disappointments, tough decisions, being battered about by people and situations I encounter, the inner calm may become dissipated. Then I need to enter another time of quiet and allow the Spirit to fill me again with the peace of Christ.

The inner calm grows with a deep trust in God. Oswald Chambers wrote about "The Theology of Rest" in his discussion of Mark 4:35-41, the story of Jesus asleep in the boat as a violent storm arose. Jesus could rest in God even in a storm. By faith we live in confidence that God is at work even in turbulent times. Chambers asked, "Are we learning to be silent before God, or are we worrying [God] with needless prayers?" Although writing in a time of war, Chambers said,

> There is no more glorious opportunity than the day in which we live for proving in personal life and in every way that we are confident in God.
>
> The stars do their work without fuss; God does His work without fuss, and saints do their work without fuss.[2]

God steadily and lovingly works at all times. God acts through saints "who because of their oneness with Him are absolutely at rest, consequently He can work through them."[3] God's gift of rest enables us to be a nonanxious presence in an anxious world.

PRAYER PRACTICE

By now you probably have a prayer word that you use every time you practice Centering Prayer. It may be a word or a sacred gaze that signals an inner turning to God or a use of the breath as a reminder of the presence of the Spirit. It is good to stay with the symbol you have chosen. Less and less do we think about the symbol itself. It becomes a subconscious part of us that comes to us naturally whenever we find ourselves engaged in some thinking. The symbol brings us into heart-space where we temporarily leave behind any thought process as we make ourselves present to God who is ever present to us. Take twenty minutes for Centering Prayer.

Read Galatians 2:19-21, allowing a word to speak to you. Meditate on that word, listening for what God is saying to you through it. How is God present for you? How do you re-present that presence to others? Pray for guidance in the ministry you have re-presenting Christ. Let the word you have received guide you in that ministry. Go forth with the inner calm of the Spirit of Christ.

37 The Gift of Letting Go

> I regard everything as loss because of the surpassing value of knowing Christ Jesus my Lord.
>
> —Philippians 3:8

I'm a "saver." I seldom throw anything away; and, to make matters worse, I like to collect things: coffee mugs, postage stamps, slides, minutes of organizations, notes from college and seminary classes, letters, newspaper clippings. I have saved childhood mementos, high school and college letters, certificates and awards. I can never destroy a book and can seldom go into a bookstore without buying one or two.

But when I retired, my wife and I moved to a smaller house. The time had come to get rid of excess baggage. We had a big garage sale. I sold and gave away many books. We let go of many material things.

Retiring, I learned another level of letting go. I stepped aside from the role of pastor, a role I had filled for forty years. It was gratifying to be able to fill that role for people, to represent the presence, comfort, and healing power of God. Through ordination the church put me in a position of ministry. I administered the sacraments of Communion and baptism. I officiated at weddings. I prayed with people who were ill. I accompanied people in grief. I walked with bewildered and lonely people.

Then I had to let go of that position and became just what I was baptized to be: a child of God, a disciple of Christ by the leading of the Holy Spirit named John David Muyskens. That is who I am. I can let go of everything else. Entering a new phase in our life journey requires letting go. We resist; but by accepting loss, we receive life.

Early in life I learned from an experience of loss. On a hike, I lost a long-desired gift my parents had given me on my twelfth birthday. That night, bringing my grief to God, I experienced a profound gift of peace. In my loss I received a greater gift.

We don't sign up for the losses that bring us to new places spiritually. They happen. Anyone who has had a life-threatening illness knows the change that comes with loss of health. Illness reshapes priorities. Loss of health, loss of a sense of invincibility, and acknowledging mortality can bring a new reliance on God.

Life is full of gains and losses. At birth we lose the comfort of the womb. At the time of weaning, we lose the security of our mother's nursing. When we receive a few items that become ours, we begin losing items as well. As we develop new relationships we also lose them. As we age and illness strikes, we lose health. And ultimately we lose our physical life in death—the ultimate letting go into the eternal love of God.

John the Baptist said of Jesus: "He must increase, but I must decrease" (John 3:30). Paul wrote to the Galatians, "It is no longer I who lives but it is Christ who lives in me" (Gal. 2:20). Jesus stated, "Those who try to make their life secure will lose it, but those who lose their life will keep it" (Luke 17:33). And he said to one young man, "Sell your possessions, and give the money to the poor; . . . then come, follow me" (Matt. 19:21).

As we relinquish ourselves, God's grace upholds us. Thomas Keating spoke at an annual conference of Contemplative Outreach about trusting the grace of God. He made a statement that struck me: "You can't lose, unless you try to win." When we strive to win, we surely lose. Letting go, we are in the arms of God.

A "welcoming prayer" is a way of embracing whatever happens and letting go. Mary Mrozowski (1925–93) originated it. In the daily round I become aware of tension or pain in my body that manifests a feeling, body sensation, emotion, or thought. At that point, I let myself sink into the sensation. Then I use the word *welcome* as a prayer word and embrace the pain or tension. I welcome God's presence and activity in it. I let go of my desire for security and approval. I give up control and release my desire to change the situation. I surrender to the love of God and the healing action of Christ.[1]

There's a story about two monks, one aged and the other a novice, walking together one morning in the monastery. The novice turned to the saintly old monk and asked, "Tell me, Father, do you still wrestle with the devil?"

"Oh, no, my son," he answered. "I'm much too old and too wise for that! You see, now I wrestle with God."

"With God?" the young novice exclaimed. "But Father, how do you hope to win?"

"Oh no, no, no, my child," said the old monk. "I hope to lose!"

PRAYER PRACTICE

Read Psalm 62:1-2. Take twenty minutes for Centering Prayer.

Read Philippians 3:7-11. Be in touch with your feelings connected with the losses you have suffered. What do you need to lose that you may "gain Christ and be found in him"? What might it mean for you to become like Christ in his death? Write what you have received as you have reflected on this scripture and what it says to you. Linger for a bit to consider the difference this meditation can make in your daily life.

38 ABANDONMENT TO DIVINE LOVE

> You have stripped off the old self with its practices and have
> clothed yourselves with the new self.
>
> —Colossians 3:9-10

People who know such things considered Michelle Kwan a strong candidate to win the gold medal in figure skating at the Winter Olympics of 2002. She won the bronze, not the gold. In an interview she said, "I spent the last year trying to reignite that light from within." At one point in her performance Kwan slipped. Sixteen-year-old Sarah Hughes, in fourth place after the initial short program, won the gold medal with an inspired performance. She later reflected, "Going into the long program I didn't think I had a chance to win gold. When I went out there, I didn't think about medals. I went out and skated for the fun of it. I didn't hold back. I just let it go." When *we* try to light the fire within we fail. In abandonment the inner light is lit.

I first read the book of talks by Jean-Pierre de Caussade (quoted in Day 34) in the translation by John Beevers. His title for the book is a phrase from de Caussade: *Abandonment to Divine Providence.* As I read, the faith de Caussade describes inspired me. How could I let go of self-concern and completely abandon myself to God's providence? Could I trust that God is at work in every moment? I began learning from de Caussade that what was required of me was to surrender to God and wait quietly in total resignation, living in love and obedience moment by moment.[1]

We like the illusion that we are in control. When a disaster strikes, such as the events of September 11, 2001, we realize the fragile nature of life. A life-threatening illness or the death of a loved one or a major disaster will let us know that actually we are *not* in control.

Over fifteen years ago, I discovered that I had a 90 percent blockage in a coronary artery; my mortality confronted me. I gained a new appreciation for the gift of life each moment. I realized in a new way that I was not in control. Life is uncertain. I have to let go of an unrealistic desire for security. Instead I can trust in the One who holds our destiny, the One who created us in love and holds us by grace.

When we surrender our lives to Christ, we have a new guide who leads us in the way of love. We enter a life of giving away the rich gifts that come to us instead of trying to hoard and control them. Our worst fears no longer take over our lives. They lose their power because we know that deeper than the greatest threats are the everlasting arms of mercy. The perfect love of Christ casts out fear.

I like to be in control. It is hard for me to release my desire for control and power. To be in the silence of Centering Prayer is an act of letting go. When I am doing the talking, I am exercising control. When I am silent, I allow God to take control.

In Centering Prayer the anxiety, pain, and sadness that reside in us are evacuated. Thomas Keating calls it "divine therapy." As we take the time to sit quietly and relax, we give our subconscious a chance to unload some of the stuff that has been deep within unattended. Memories of past hurts and disappointments can come to us. When pain or grief or anger emerges, it can be unloaded. It is evacuated as we return to the sacred word. This evacuation is a healthy exercise that brings inner healing. In rare moments we become aware of a matter that needs some attention outside the prayer period. After the prayer period we may journal about it or talk with a trusted counselor. Usually a gentle letting go allows the "divine therapy" to work in us.

When we hold on to hatred, bitterness, shame, or anxiety, it corrodes our souls. Healing comes as we let go of these negative emotions.

Letting go of all that keeps us from God, we let God make us whole. Stripped of the old self, we are clothed with the love and peace of Christ.

PRAYER PRACTICE

Once again let your breathing symbolize your openness to God and your letting go of every obstacle to intimacy with God. Breathe deeply and slowly. As you inhale imagine that you are inviting the Spirit of God to transform you. Imagine as you exhale that you are letting go of every hindrance to a close relationship with God. Give twenty minutes to Centering Prayer.

Read Colossians 3:5-15. What does this text say to you? Take an inventory. What needs to be discarded to be rid of the old self? Write in your journal. What qualities of the true self are you called to put on? Ask for the willingness to be transformed. Decide what "clothing" you will wear as you enter your daily relationships and activities.

39 CONTEMPLATION AND ACTION

Those who abide in love abide in God, and God abides in them.
—1 John 4:16

At one time I equated contemplation with inaction. Really it enhances the work we do and leads us into active ministry.

Work goes best when done in a contemplative mode. I call it contemplative work. This insight came to me while doing the tedious labor of mowing my lawn. When I became anxious to get the job done and acted hastily, the effort did not go well. When I decided to apply my understandings from contemplative prayer, I entered the work with more attention to what I was doing. Instead of anxiously awaiting the end of the task, I entered into the joy of doing it and doing it as well as I could. A contemplative attitude makes tedious work more enjoyable. Sawing a board becomes a moment to appreciate the cut of the saw and to celebrate the beauty of the grain of the wood. Washing the dishes becomes a moment of gratitude for clean dishes and good meals. Every task becomes an opportunity to share in the activity of God. Far from taking me out of the world of work, contemplation gives me a way to enter into it fully. I become more aware of reality rather than escaping from it.

I now apply a contemplative attitude to driving. Of course, I must remain alert when driving, but being contemplative does not mean lack of attentiveness. Just the opposite, it increases our attentiveness without the anxiety that sometimes accompanies the effort to concentrate. When I drove long distances I would set my mind on the destination and measure each mile by how much farther I had to drive. The anxiety over reaching the end of the trip increased as I went along, so the last miles were agonizing. I would be getting closer but still had miles to go.

I have come to realize that being on the journey can be fun. On the journey I can look at scenery, notice other cars and trucks, listen to the radio or a recording, talk with others in the car—I can enjoy the moment. I can be content with where I am while moving toward my destination. Being contemplative on the journey makes the trip itself a joy.

The practice of Centering Prayer leads us into active ministry. Contemplation gives us deep peace and, at the same time, deep disturbance. It opens us in love to the suffering of the world as well as to its joy and beauty. Contemplative prayer will take us to places of solitude and company. Together we become companions in the journey, standing with those who suffer. In seeking to share the gospel, we move from the center to the periphery where the redemptive love of Christ embraces those on the margins.

Contemplative prayer does not consist of petitions. But it is not in any opposition to petitionary prayer. In contemplative prayer without words, we enter the compassion of God. We pray with Christ on the cross. We enter into the pain of God's sorrow over the brokenness of our world. Our prayer arises out of God's love, so it bears the pain of all the sin and alienation, illness and death that is so much a part of our human experience. With consent to the presence and action of God, we intercede for all creation. We join in all the prayers of people everywhere and participate in God's redemptive work. We become agents of God's grace.

In contemplative prayer we acknowledge the nearness of the kingdom of God, within and around us, which becomes visible to us through the eyes of faith. Contemplation helps us see with sharper focus the needs of humanity. We realize that our blessings are invitations to participate in God's work by relieving the pain of others. We do our part in making the world a community of justice and peace.

Thomas Merton's experience on a busy corner of Louisville gave him an overwhelming realization of unity with all the people. A love for them welled up in him. He says he woke from a dream of isolation to see the beauty and depth at the core of each person. He knew the world could change if people only saw themselves and others through God's eyes.[1]

For Merton compassion is the stream that flows from the spring of contemplation.

PRAYER PRACTICE

Be aware of your feelings at the moment. Notice any place of tension in your body. Take note of the tense feeling there and then let go of it. Breathe in deeply, taking in the peace and love of Christ. As you exhale let go of the anxieties that you are holding within. Do twenty minutes of Centering Prayer.

Read 1 John 4:16-21. Let a word in the text attract your attention. Listen to what it says to you. What does it mean for the way you live in the world, the way you do your work, the way you relate to other people? How can you share the love of God? Bring any concerns that arise to God, lifting them to God and listening for any further word. Settle into a contemplative attitude that you can bring into your round of activity.

40 Contemplation and Community

The fruit of the Spirit is love, joy, peace, patience, kindness. . . .
—Galatians 5:22

The prophetic question a physician asked me some years ago, "Are you trying to do it all yourself?" set me on a new path. I needed the nurture of a regular practice of prayer in order to do what I was called to do. I found the discipline of Centering Prayer. The people who knew me as their pastor sensed a new passion in me. The congregation became a community of encouragement in the spiritual journey. In our meetings we gave more time to prayer and listening to scripture. These spiritual disciplines sustained and equipped us for ministry. As we continued to be engaged in ministries of compassion, they flowed from the wells that were being filled by prayer and worship.

In Centering Prayer we enter into the love of God expressed as a yearning for the wholeness of all creation. We then cooperate with God's will that is "set forth in Christ, as a plan for the fullness of time, to gather up all things in him, things in heaven and things on earth" (Eph. 1:9-10).

Jesus said, "Let your light shine before others, so that they may see your good works and give glory to your Father in heaven" (Matt. 5:16). We can be like a prism. As we receive the light of Christ, it can shine through us. It comes out in a rainbow of color: love, joy, peace, patience, kindness, generosity, faithfulness, gentleness, and self-control (Gal. 5:22).

Our world desperately needs to know its true Center. People need to experience the love of the Source of life in whom we live each day. Our fractured world is in grave danger of destroying itself. We are called to point to God who has the grace and power to draw all things together. We become part of the mission of Christ to create "one new humanity" (Eph. 2:15).

The word for justice in Hebrew, *tsedakah*, means having a right attitude toward God, others, and self. Out of a deepening relationship with God, we will work for justice in human relationships.

Justice can usher in peace, shalom. Shalom means well-being and has many dimensions: harmony with God and with all creation; grateful awareness of the grace and providence in which we live; the deep peace the world so desperately needs; the well-being out of which we offer kindness rather than hostility. A deep sense of God's love transforms us into people of love.

In his opposition to Nazism, Dietrich Bonhoeffer knew the value of life together in Christ. He taught the students in his Preacher's Seminary that solitude and silence were necessary not only for their own enrichment but for building community.[1]

To a superficial observer the practice of Centering Prayer may seem to be private, centered only in self. Quite the opposite is true. It draws us into community, never bringing us to solitary stillness and leaving us there. Never a selfish endeavor, it brings us to God, Creator of all, and connects us with all creation.

Centering Prayer draws us into the love of the divine community: Father, Son, and Holy Spirit. United with the source of all, we are one with all that is. United with Christ we participate in Christ's passion for all humanity. United in the Spirit we are filled with compassion for all. The Trinity's hospitality brings us into unity with all God's children.

The Rublev icon of the Trinity beautifully portrays the gift of hospitality. In it we see the three messengers who come to Abraham and Sarah at the oak of Mamre. The picture recalls the hospitality Abraham and Sarah offer their visitors. The visitors appear as angels who, for Rublev, represent the Father, Son, and Holy Spirit. They sit at a table with the front side open, inviting us to come and share in the meal of lamb. The rectangular box in the front of the table, like a reliquary reminding worshipers of the martyrs and saints of the past, invites us to join all the people of faith. The hospitality of the Trinity welcomes us to the table with them.

The love of the Trinity, far from isolating us, leads to compassion. It heightens awareness of the presence of God in other people. It brings us into an open and inviting community, filling us with a love that calls us to hospitality.

A network of people called Contemplative Outreach supports the practice of Centering Prayer. Their goal is "to live ordinary life with extraordinary love." The vision statement of Contemplative Outreach calls itself a "network of individuals and small faith communities committed to living the contemplative dimension of the Gospel in everyday life through the practice of Centering Prayer. The contemplative dimension of the

Gospel manifests itself in an ever-deepening union with the living Christ and the practical caring for others that flows from that relationship."

PRAYER PRACTICE

Read Psalm 67. Give twenty minutes to Centering Prayer, while letting the wonder of God's love fill you.

Read Galatians 5:22-26. Take a word from the reading and listen to its message for you. Write what you hear. In prayer ask the Spirit to point the way you are called to serve God. How are you to participate in God's work in the world? What have you learned in these forty days about the practice of prayer and scripture meditation that will continue to sustain you? What are the Spirit's invitations for you?

You can continue with daily scripture meditation by using a lectionary of daily Bible readings or by working your way through a book of the Bible. For *lectio divina* choose short portions, allowing a word or short phrase to speak to you and meditating on that. By now you know that a regular practice of Centering Prayer will produce a daily harvest of grace. It will help you live ordinary life with extraordinary love.

SUGGESTIONS FOR GROUP STUDY

It is intended that each group member be reading the book and following the suggested practices *before* the first meeting. If a preliminary meeting is desired, someone who has gone through the book or is familiar with Centering Prayer can present the book and have members of the group introduce themselves to one another. There can be some sharing of experience with prayer and the felt need for spiritual practices, either one-on-one or as a group.

The group gatherings are designed for a once-a-week meeting. On the day of the meeting the members may use the group meeting as a time for Centering Prayer and skip that day's reading. This approach can work well in Lent if the meetings are on Sunday, because Sundays are not included in the forty days of Lent. Then Ash Wednesday can be the first day and forty readings done on the forty weekdays of Lent. In any case, group members need to receive instruction about the plan for reading as they begin.

FIRST MEETING

Sit in a circle with a symbol at the center such as a candle, a cross, or a Bible. The leader will ask participants to breathe deeply, imagining their openness to receive the presence of God with each inhalation and letting go of every obstacle to receiving God's presence with each exhalation.

With a volunteer serving as timer, be in silence for twenty minutes for Centering Prayer. The timer may begin with a short verbal prayer giving thanks for God's presence and asking for help in letting go of ordinary concerns for the time of prayer. An example is the prayer used by a group in Milwaukee to open their time of Centering Prayer. (See Appendix 1, page 125.) The timer may end the twenty minutes with the Lord's Prayer, offering it slowly and softly, not in unison. The leader or timer should announce before the prayer period that the Lord's Prayer will not be said in unison.

Then John 15:1-5 or another passage can be chosen for group *lectio divina*. (See Appendix 3 on group *lectio*, page 127.)

After the *lectio* the leader can invite everyone to share with one other person what has been happening for him or her while following the daily meditations.

As time allows, discuss in the entire group how spending time in silence has gone. Remember that Centering Prayer is not clearing the mind of thoughts. It is a method of letting go of thoughts by turning to God using a prayer word that expresses the intention of consenting to God's presence and action within.

SECOND MEETING

After two weeks of exploring contemplative prayer, meet again as a group for prayer and sharing. Praying silently in a group can be a profound experience. It has a dimension that solitary prayer does not have. Jesus promised, "Where two or three are gathered in my name, I am there among them" (Matt. 18:20).

Again, someone will be the timer for twenty minutes of silence for Centering Prayer, beginning with a verbal prayer such as the one in Appendix 1 and ending with the Lord's Prayer offered slowly and quietly, not in unison.

Read Luke 10:38-42. You can use the group *lectio* method (Appendix 3, page 127), or the leader can ask members to imagine themselves in the story as it is read, seeing, hearing, smelling, feeling the scene. The leader can guide a meditation by asking everyone, with eyes closed, to enter the scene and see Mary, Martha, and Jesus as it is read slowly again. The leader will ask the participants to imagine the feelings of each of the three. Then the leader will ask that participants be there as one of the disciples and will raise this question: How do you feel as you observe what happens? Speak with one other person about that experience. Talk with that person about how you can "sit at the feet of Jesus."

Share with the group experiences with contemplative prayer. Talk about time and place for Centering Prayer.

THIRD MEETING

The group gathering begins with twenty minutes of Centering Prayer. The timer may begin with a verbal prayer asking that the group be given an openness to the presence of God and be allowed to let go of concerns in order to be with God in faith and love. The timer's offering of the Lord's Prayer slowly and quietly may close the twenty minutes.

Group *lectio* can be used with Matthew 6:5-8, Jesus' teachings on prayer.

Then invite sharing about the experience of practicing Centering Prayer. The participants may speak about what struck them from the daily readings and scripture texts. They may then lift up verbal prayers that grow out of the discussion and prayers for needs brought to the group.

FOURTH MEETING

The group will again gather for mutual support and encouragement. Centering Prayer may begin with the leader's offering a brief prayer and a quote from a psalm or other reading. After twenty minutes of Centering Prayer, the leader may slowly offer the Lord's Prayer (not recited in unison).

With Ephesians 3:14-19 as the text, use the group *lectio* way of reflection. Here is a variation on the group *lectio* outlined in Appendix 3: After the text is read twice and time allowed for silent meditation, participants are invited to say out loud the word that spoke to their heart. After another reading and silence, the participants are invited to share a sentence or two of what has come to them in the silence. After a fourth reading the participants are invited to offer aloud prayers that grow out of their meditation.

If time remains, group members may share experiences of the past week.

FIFTH MEETING

The group can gather again, now after five weeks of experience with Centering Prayer. A person who will be the timer for the twenty minutes of Centering Prayer can begin with a prayer that hearts may be open to God and conclude the prayer period by slowly offering the Lord's Prayer.

A group *lectio* reading of 1 John 4:16-21 can be done.

Then give time to faith sharing out of the practice of Centering Prayer. How is the practice making a difference in the participants' lives?

SIXTH MEETING AND BEYOND

A Bible reading is chosen before the meeting. Begin with a time of Centering Prayer. Then the scripture passage can be read, and the group can engage in *lectio divina*.

There may be some discussion about continuing a prayer group that will support its members in their practice of prayer and in meeting the challenges of following Christ in their various situations. Numerous options abound. You can simply meet for Centering Prayer and faith sharing. You can pray with scripture using the group *lectio* method. You can read and discuss a book on Centering Prayer or view videotapes that are available through Contemplative Outreach. (See Appendix 4, page 128.)

Appendix 1: Milwaukee Benediction

Father, Son and Holy Spirit,
Creator, Redeemer, Sanctifier,
Alive at the Center of our being,
We wish to surrender in love to you.

May our sacred word,
Which we will use whenever
we become engaged with anything else,
Be a sign and a symbol of our intention
to consent to your divine presence and action
within.

Used as the opening prayer for every Centering Prayer period by a group in Milwaukee.

Appendix 2: Guidelines for Leaders

Welcome the participants.

Read the guidelines, especially for any who are new to Centering Prayer. Announce how the prayer period will begin and end and the length of time. Usually the time period will be twenty minutes. A bell can mark the beginning and end of the prayer period, or the silent time can begin with the prayer below and end with the Lord's Prayer or spontaneous prayer by the leader. If using the Lord's Prayer announce that the leader will offer it to close, and all are to listen.

Guidelines of Centering Prayer

1. Choose a sacred word as the symbol of your intention to consent to God's presence and action within.

2. Sitting comfortably and with eyes closed, settle briefly and silently introduce the sacred word as the symbol of your consent to God's presence and action within.

3. When engaged with your thoughts, return ever-so-gently to the sacred word.

4. At the end of the prayer period, remain in silence with eyes closed for a couple of minutes.

Use the following prayer or another in the leader's own words:

> Source of All, Savior, Holy Spirit:
> We welcome your presence at the center of our being.
> Letting go of all else, we surrender in love to you.
> Let our sacred word be a symbol of our consent to your loving presence and healing action within.

Twenty minutes of silence

Offering of the Lord's Prayer slowly and quietly by the leader. Or free prayer offered by the leader.

Appendix 3: Group Lectio

For many centuries people employed a method called *lectio divina* to listen to God though words of the Bible. Especially used in monasteries, it is increasingly being discovered as a significant way of praying with scripture. In *lectio* you listen for what God is saying to you.

Group Lectio

When the group uses the *lectio divina* way of scripture meditation, consider the following outline. The leader will read the passage and invite a response four times.

Before the first reading, ask participants to let one word emerge in their consciousness. Tell them to take just one word that stands out. It may help to hear the first reading twice. After a time of silence, say, "Now, if you wish, you may speak out loud the word that came to you from the reading."

After allowing enough time for those who wish to speak a word, introduce the second reading by encouraging participants to reflect on the word they have received and by announcing that they will have the opportunity to share a sentence or two that grows out of their reflection. Invite participants to consider these questions: What is the Spirit saying to me, and how does it apply to my life? Read the text and allow a time of silence for meditation on the word received. Then say, "Now, if you wish, you may speak a sentence or two that comes out of your reflection in the silence."

Before the third reading, announce that after this reading there will be a time for prayer that arises out of the time of meditation and other concerns the group members would like to lift up to God. After the third reading, allow a time for silent prayer. Then invite the participants to voice their prayers in response to the word received or any concern on their hearts.

Before the fourth reading, tell the group that the silence after the reading is to let the word sink in and get ready to take it with you. Draw this time to a close with a brief prayer of thanksgiving or, if the Lord's Prayer was not used earlier, the group can offer it together.

Appendix 4: Encouragement

We often need encouragement in the practice of Centering Prayer. Happily we are not alone in the practice. Resources are available to us.

You can learn more about Centering Prayer by reading *Open Mind, Open Heart: The Contemplative Dimension of the Gospel* by Thomas Keating and other books by Thomas Keating and Basil Pennington.

You can find others who practice Centering Prayer in your area by contacting the network that supports Centering Prayer called Contemplative Outreach. Their international office is at 10 Park Place, Suite 2-B, Butler, NJ 07405. E-mail: office@coutreach.org. Web site: www.contemplativeoutreach.org. A coordinator in your area can help locate workshops and prayer groups available.

NOTES

DAY 3 THE INNER FLAME OF THE SPIRIT

1. *Living Flame of Love*, in *The Complete Works of Saint John of the Cross*, trans. E. Allison Peers (London: Burns Oates & Washbourne, 1953), 3:18.

DAY 5 LETTING GOD SET THE PACE

1. See *Calvin: Institutes of the Christian Religion*, ed. John T. McNeill, trans. Ford Lewis Battles, Library of Christian Classics, vol. 21 (Philadelphia, Pa.: Westminster Press, 1960), 41.

DAY 7 THE METHOD OF CENTERING PRAYER

1. *The Cloud of Unknowing*, ed. James Walsh (New York: Paulist Press, 1981), 134.

DAY 9 A PROPHET'S INSIGHT

1. A. W. Tozer, *The Pursuit of God* (Camp Hill, Pa.: Christian Publications, 1993), 7.
2. Ibid., xvi.
3. Ibid., xvii.
4. A. W. Tozer, "Man: the Dwelling Place of God," in *The Best of A. W. Tozer*, comp. Warren W. Wiersbe (Grand Rapids, Mich.: Baker Book House, 1978), 161.
5. Ibid., 162.
6. *The Pursuit of God*, 7.
7. Ibid., 9.

DAY 12 AN OVERFLOWING CHALICE

1. *The Pursuit of God*, 11–12.
2. Gerald G. May, *Addiction and Grace* (San Francisco: Harper & Row, Publishers, 1988), 1.

DAY 13 SILENCE

1. Thomas à Kempis, *Of the Imitation of Christ* (New Kensington, Pa.: Whitaker House, 1981), 41–43.

DAY 15 PRAYER IN THE EARLY CHURCH

1. *John Cassian: The Conferences*, trans. Boniface Ramsey (New York: Paulist Press, 1997), 381.
2. *The Philokalia: The Complete Text*, comp. St. Nikodimos of the Holy Mountain and St. Makarios of Corinth, trans. and ed. by G. E. H. Palmer, Philip Sherrard, and Kallistos Ware (London: Faber and Faber, 1983), 1:42.
3. Ibid., 64-68.
4. Ibid., 163–97.

DAY 16 CENTERING PRAYER IN CHRISTIAN HISTORY

1. *Writings from the Philokalia on Prayer of the Heart*, trans. E. Kadloubovsky and G. E. H. Palmer (London: Faber and Faber, 1992), 74–76.
2. *The Cloud of Unknowing*, ed. James Walsh (New York: Paulist Press, 1981), 119.
3. Ibid., 125.
4. Ibid., 128.
5. Ibid.
6. Ibid., 133–34.

DAY 17 THOUGHTS

1. Oswald Chambers, *My Utmost for His Highest* (Uhrichsville, Ohio: Barbour and Company, 1963), August 23.
2. *Calvin: Institutes*, 853–54.
3. Ibid., 54.
4. John Calvin, *The Epistles of Paul the Apostle to the Galatians, Ephesians, Philippians, and Colossians*, trans. T. H. L. Parker, eds. David W. Torrance and Thomas F. Torrance, Calvin's Commentaries (Grand Rapids, Mich.: William B. Eerdmans Publishing Company, 1965), 289.

DAY 18 PRAYER TOO DEEP FOR WORDS

1. Howard Thurman, *The Centering Moment* (New York: Harper & Row, Publishers, 1969.

2. Frank C. Laubach, *Prayer: The Mightiest Force in the World* (Westwood, N.J.: Fleming H. Revell Company, 1959), 31.

3. Ibid., 81.

DAY 20 FOUNTAIN OF RESTORATION

1. *The Life of the Holy Mother Teresa of Jesus*, in *The Complete Works of Saint Teresa of Jesus*, trans. E. Allison Peers (London: Sheed and Ward, 1950), 1:62–111.

2. Ibid., 111.

3. Ibid., 112.

DAY 21 THE LORD'S INNER CHAMBER

1. Teresa of Ávila, *Interior Castle*, in *The Complete Works of Saint Teresa of Jesus*, 2:187–351.

2. Ibid., 247.

3. Ibid., 248.

4. Ibid., 269.

5. Ibid., 276–77.

6. Ibid., 276.

7. Ibid., 331.

8. Ibid., 332.

9. Ibid.

10. Ibid., 334.

11. Ibid., 335.

DAY 22 GOD'S DWELLING AT THE CENTER

1. Oswald Chambers, *The Place of Help: God's Provision for Our Daily Needs* (Grand Rapids, Mich.: Discovery House Publishers, 1989), 167.

2. Ibid., 168.

DAY 23 OUR MYSTICAL UNION WITH CHRIST

1. John Calvin, *The Second Epistle of Paul the Apostle to the Corinthians and the Epistles to Timothy, Titus and Philemon*, trans. T. A. Smail, eds. David W. Torrance and Thomas F. Torrance, Calvin's Commentaries (Grand Rapids, Mich.: William B. Eerdmans Publishing Company, 1964), 91.

2. John Calvin, *The Epistles of Paul the Apostle to the Romans and to the Thessalonians*, trans. Ross MacKenzie, eds. David W. Torrance and Thomas F. Torrance, Calvin's Commentaries (Grand Rapids, Mich.: William B. Eerdmans Publishing Company, 1961), 165.

3. Calvin, *Ephesians*, 167–68.

4. *Calvin: Institutes*, 737.

5. *Calvin: Institutes*, 473.

6. *Calvin: Institutes*, 570-71.

7. *Calvin: Institutes*, 1373.

DAY 26 INTIMATE COMMUNION

1. Bernard of Clairvaux, *Sermons on the Song of Songs*, vol. 4, trans. Irene Edmonds, Cistercian Fathers Series (Kalamazoo, Mich.: Cistercian Publications, 1980), 191–92.

2. Ibid., 208–209.

3. *Calvin: Institutes*, 890.

4. Ibid., 854.

5. Thomas à Kempis, *Of the Imitation of Christ*, 44.

6. Ibid., 63.

DAY 27 PRAYER OF THE HEART

1. *Calvin: Institutes*, 852.

2. I. John Hesselink, *Calvin's First Catechism: A Commentary*, trans. Ford Lewis Battles (Louisville, Ky.: Westminster John Knox Press, 1997), 28.

3. *Calvin: Institutes*, 857.

4. Ibid., 891–92.

5. *Institutes*, 892.

6. Ibid.

7. Theophan the Recluse in *The Art of Prayer: An Orthodox Anthology,* comp. Igumen Chariton of Valamo, trans. Elizabeth M. Palmer (London: Faber and Faber, 1966), 110.

Day 28 Prayer as Receptivity

1. *Calvin: Institutes,* 856.
2. Ibid., 859.
3. Ibid., 862.
4. Ibid., 865.

Day 29 Moving to Another Level

1. *Dark Night of the Soul,* in *The Complete Works of Saint John of the Cross,* rev. ed., trans. E. Allison Peers (London: Burns Oates & Washbourne, 1953), 349.
2. Ibid., 354.
3. Ibid., 386.
4. Ibid., 456–57.
5. Ibid., 355.
6. *Living Flame of Love* in *The Complete Works of Saint John of the Cross,* 158.
7. Ibid., 161.
8. Ibid., 177.
9. Ibid., 178.
10. Ibid., 178–79.
11. Saint John of the Cross, *Dark Night of the Soul,* 404.

Day 30 Living Out of the Center

1. *The Breath of Life: A Simple Way to Pray,* by Ron DelBene with Mary and Herb Montgomery (Nashville, Tenn.: Upper Room Books, 1992).

DAY 31 DAILY PRAYER

1. Jane Redmont, *When in Doubt Sing: Experiencing Prayer in Everyday Life* (New York: Harper Collins Publishers, 1999), 325–26.
2. *Calvin: Institutes*, 888.
3. Ibid., 917–18.
4. Ibid., 892.
5. George W. Noble, ed., *Book of Prayers for Everybody and for All Occasions* (Chicago: Geo. W. Noble, Publisher, 1907), 126.

DAY 34 THE GIFT OF THE PRESENT MOMENT

1. In notes by John Varineau in the Grand Rapids Symphony 2001–2002 season playbill, 67.
2. Jean-Pierre de Caussade, *The Sacrament of the Present Moment*, trans. Kitty Muggeridge (San Francisco: HarperSanFrancisco, 1989), 11.

DAY 35 THE MOUNTAIN IS OUT

1. "The Elixir," *The Works of George Herbert in Prose and Verse* (New York: John Wurtele Lovell, 1881), 288–89.
2. Chambers, *My Utmost for His Highest*, July 20.

DAY 36 RE-PRESENTING CHRIST

1. Paul Lawson, "Systems Theory and Centering Prayer" in *Centering Prayer in Daily Life and Ministry*, ed. Gustave Reininger (New York: Continuum, 1998), 89.
2. Chambers, *The Place of Help*, 49–50.
3. Ibid.

DAY 37 THE GIFT OF LETTING GO

1. See Thomas Keating, *Open Mind, Open Heart: The Contemplative Dimension of the Gospel* (New York: Continuum, 1992), 124–25 and Cynthia Bourgeault, *Centering Prayer and Inner Awakening* (Cambridge, Mass.: Cowley Publications, 2004), 150–51.

DAY 38 ABANDONMENT TO DIVINE LOVE

1. Jean-Pierre de Caussade, *Abandonment to Divine Providence*, trans. John Beevers (New York: Image Books, 1975), 59.

DAY 39 CONTEMPLATION AND ACTION

1. Thomas Merton, *Conjectures of a Guilty Bystander* (Garden City, N.Y.: Doubleday & Co., 1966), 140.

DAY 40 CONTEMPLATION AND COMMUNITY

1. Dietrich Bonhoeffer, *Life Together; Prayerbook of the Bible*, ed. Geffrey B. Kelly, trans. Daniel W. Bloesch and James H. Burtness (Minneapolis, Minn.: Fortress Press, 1996).

BIBLIOGRAPHY

Bourgeault, Cynthia. *Centering Prayer and Inner Awakening.* Cambridge, Mass.: Cowley Publications, 2004.

Calvin, John. *Calvin: Institutes of the Christian Religion.* Vol. 21. Ed. John T. McNeill. Trans. Ford Lewis Battles. Philadelphia, Pa.: The Westminster Press, 1960.

Cloud of Unknowing, The. Ed. William Johnston. New York: Image Books, 1973.

De Caussade, Jean-Pierre, *Abandonment to Divine Providence.* Trans. John Beevers. New York: Image Books, 1975.

_____. *The Sacrament of the Present Moment.* Trans. Kitty Muggeridge. San Francisco: HarperSanFrancisco, 1989.

Edwards, Tilden H. *Living in the Presence: Spiritual Exercises to Open Our Lives to the Awareness of God.* New York: HarperCollins, 1995.

John of the Cross. *Living Flame of Love.* Trans. and ed. E. Allison Peers. New York: Triumph Books, 1991.

Keating, Thomas. *Open Mind, Open Heart: The Contemplative Dimension of the Gospel.* New York: Continuum International Publishing Group, 2002.

_____. *Intimacy with God: An Introduction to Centering Prayer.* New York: Crossroad Publishing Company, 1994.

Lawson, Paul David. *Old Wine in New Skins: Centering Prayer and Systems Theory.* New York: Lantern Books, 2001.

Pennington, M. Basil. *Centered Living: The Way of Centering Prayer.* Liguori, Mo.: Liguori Publications, 1999.

Peterson, Eugene H. *Working the Angles: The Shape of Pastoral Integrity.* Grand Rapids, Mich.: William B. Eerdmans Publishing Company, 1987.

Postema, Don. *Space for God: Study and Practice of Spirituality and Prayer.* Grand Rapids, Mich.: CRC Publications, 1997.

Reininger, Gustave, ed. *Centering Prayer in Daily Life and Ministry*. New York: Continuum, 1998.

Teresa of Avila. *A Life of Prayer, Faith and Passion for God Alone*. Ed. James M. Houston. Minneapolis, Mn.: Bethany House Publishers, 1983.

Tozer, Aiden Wilson. *The Pursuit of God*. Camp Hill, Pa.: Christian Publications, Inc., 1993.

About the Author

J. David Muyskens, a retired minister of the Reformed Church in America and a seminary teacher of spirituality, holds a Doctor of Ministry degree from Princeton Theological Seminary. He has been a spiritual director since 1991 and is a graduate of the Spiritual Guidance Program of the Shalem Institute in Bethesda, Maryland. He has been practicing Centering Prayer daily since 1993 and has facilitated a Centering Prayer group since 2001.

Reverend Muyskens was commissioned by Contemplative Outreach as a presenter of the Introductory Centering Prayer Workshop in 1999. He was appointed coordinator of a newly formed chapter of Contemplative Outreach in West Michigan in November of 2002 and has served in that capacity since. He is currently a member of the Circle of Service of Contemplative Outreach as the Coordinator of the International Service Team. He has authored several books and numerous articles.

Reverend Muyskens is married, has a son, two daughters, and five grandchildren. His other interests include genealogy pursuits and wood carving.

ANOTHER BOOK BY J. DAVID MUYSKENS

Sacred Breath: Forty Days of Centering Prayer

Centering Prayer is a powerful prayer practice. For people interested in silent prayer and those practicing Centering Prayer already, this book supports their discipline with practical and encouraging content. The daily readings and outline for group sessions also will help individuals maintain the practice for forty days. Having practiced the discipline for this period of time, people will be more inclined and able to continue Centering Prayer.

UPPER ROOM BOOKS OF RELATED INTEREST

Dimensions of Prayer: Cultivating a Relationship with God
by Douglas V. Steere

Gathered in the Word: Praying the Scripture in Small Groups
by Norvene Vest

Heart Whispers: Benedictine Wisdom for Today
by Elizabeth J. Canham

Praying in the Wesleyan Spirit: 52 Prayers for Today
by Paul Wesley Chilcote

Shaped by the Word: The Power of Scripture in Spiritual Formation
by M. Robert Mulholland Jr.

Talking in the Dark: Praying When Life Doesn't Make Sense
by Steve Harper

Teach Me to Pray
by W. E. Sangster